Dedication

Moaz Safi Yousef al-Kasasbeh
May 29, 1988–January 3, 2015

Also by Yatir Nitzany

Conversational Portuguese Quick and Easy

....

Conversational Spanish Quick and Easy

....

Conversational Italian Quick and Easy

....

Conversational French Quick and Easy

....

Conversational German Quick and Easy

....

Conversational Russian Quick and Easy

....

Conversational Polish Quick and Easy

....

Conversational Hebrew Quick and Easy

....

Conversational Yiddish Quick and Easy

....

Conversational Arabic Quick and Easy
Classical Arabic

....

Conversational Arabic Quick and Easy
Palestinian Dialect

....

Conversational Arabic Quick and Easy
Egyptian Dialect

....

Conversational Arabic Quick and Easy
Jordanian Dialect

....

Conversational Arabic Quick and Easy
Emirati Dialect

....

Conversational Arabic Quick and Easy
Syrian Dialect

Conversational
Arabic
Quick and Easy

SAUDI DIALECTS

YATIR NITZANY

Printed in the United States of America

Foreword

About Myself

For many years I struggled to learn Spanish, and I still knew no more than about twenty words. Consequently, I was extremely frustrated. One day I stumbled upon this method as I was playing around with word combinations. Suddenly, I came to the realization that every language has a certain core group of words that are most commonly used and, simply by learning them, one could gain the ability to engage in quick and easy conversational Spanish.

I discovered which words those were, and I narrowed them down to three hundred and fifty that, once memorized, one could connect and create one's own sentences. The variations were and are infinite! By using this incredibly simple technique, I could converse at a proficient level and speak Spanish. Within a week, I astonished my Spanish-speaking friends with my newfound ability. The next semester I registered at my university for a Spanish language course, and I applied the same principles I had learned in that class (grammar, additional vocabulary, future and past tense, etc.) to those three hundred and fifty words I already had memorized, and immediately I felt as if I had grown wings and learned how to fly.

At the end of the semester, we took a class trip to San José, Costa Rica. I was like a fish in water, while the rest of my classmates were floundering and still struggling to converse. Throughout the following months, I again applied the same principle to other languages—French, Portuguese, Italian, and Arabic, all of which I now speak proficiently, thanks to this very simple technique.

This method is by far the fastest way to master quick and easy conversational language skills. There is no other technique that compares to my concept. It is effective, it worked for me, and it will work for you. Be consistent with my program, and you too will succeed the way I and many, many others have.

Contents

INTRODUCTION TO
THE PROGRAM

People often dream about learning a foreign language, but usually they never do it. Some feel that they just won't be able to do it while others believe that they don't have the time. Whatever your reason is, it's time to set that aside. With my new method, you will have enough time, and you will not fail. You will actually learn how to speak the fundamentals of the language—fluently in as little as a few days. Of course, you won't speak perfect the Najdi, Hijazi, or the Saudi Gulf dialects at first, but you will certainly gain significant proficiency. For example, if you travel to the Saudi Arabia Peninsula, you will almost effortlessly be able engage in basic conversational communication with the locals in the present tense and you will no longer be intimidated by culture shock. It's time to relax. Learning a language is a valuable skill that connects people of multiple cultures around the world—and you now have the tools to join them.

How does my method work? I have taken twenty-seven of the most commonly used languages in the world and distilled from them the three hundred and fifty most frequently used words in any language. This process took three years of observation and research, and during that time, I determined which words I felt were most important for this method of basic conversational communication. In that time, I chose these words in such a way that they were structurally interrelated and that, when combined, form sentences. Thus, once you succeed in memorizing these words, you will be able to combine these words and form your own sentences. The words are spread over twenty pages. The words will also combine easily in sentences, for example, enabling you to ask simple questions, make basic statements, and obtain a rudimentary understanding of others' communications. I have also created Memorization Made Easy techniques for this program in order to help with the memorization of the vocabulary. Please also see Reading and Pronunciation of Arabic accents in order to gain proficiency in the reading and pronunciation of the Arabic language prior to starting this program. Please also see Reading and Pronunciation of Arabic accents in order to gain proficiency in the reading and pronunciation of the Arabic language prior to starting this program.

My book is mainly intended for basic present tense vocal communication, meaning anyone can easily use it to "get by" linguistically while visiting a foreign country without learning the entire language. With practice, you will be 100 percent understandable to native speakers, which is your aim. One disclaimer: this is not a grammar book, though it does address minute and essential grammar rules. Therefore, understanding complex sentences with obscure words in Arabic is beyond the scope of this book.

People who have tried this method have been successful, and by the time you finish this book, you will understand and be understood in basic conversational Arabic. This is the best basis to learn not only the Arabic language but any language. This is an entirely revolutionary, no-fail concept, and your ability to combine the pieces of the "language puzzle" together will come with great ease, especially if you use this program prior to beginning an Arabic class.

This is the best program that was ever designed to teach the reader how to become conversational. Other conversational programs will only teach you phrases. But this is the only program that will teach you how to create your own sentences for the purpose of becoming conversational.

MEMORIZATION MADE EASY

There is no doubt the three hundred and fifty words in my program are the required essentials in order to engage in quick and easy basic conversation in any foreign language. However, some people may experience difficulty in the memorization. For this reason, I created Memorization Made Easy. This memorization technique will make this program so simple and fun that it's unbelievable! I have spread the words over the following twenty pages. Each page contains a vocabulary table of ten to fifteen words. Below every vocabulary box, sentences are composed from the words on the page that you have just studied. This aids greatly in memorization. Once you succeed in memorizing the first page, then proceed to the second page. Upon completion of the second page, go back to the first and review. Then proceed to the third page. After memorizing the third, go back to the first and second and repeat. And so on. As you continue, begin to combine words and create your own sentences in your head. Every time you proceed to the following page, you will notice words from the previous pages will be present in those simple sentences as well, because repetition is one of the most crucial aspects in learning any foreign language. Upon completion of your twenty pages, congratulations, you have absorbed the required words and gained a basic, quick-and-easy proficiency and you should now be able to create your own sentences and say anything you wish in the Najdi Arabic dialect. This is a crash course in conversational Arabic, and it works!

Conversational
Arabic Quick
and Easy

SAUDI NAJDI DIALECT

YATIR NITZANY

The Najdi Arabic Dialect

The current population of Saudi Arabia is estimated at 32.94 million (2017). As with most Arabic countries, Modern Standard Arabic (MSA) is the formal version of the language but mainly used in newspapers, books, and the media. It is taught in schools as a secondary language.

Apart from MSA, there are three distinct dialects of Arabic within the country. There is the Hejazi Dialect, Gulf Arabic and Najdi Arabic. Najdi Arabic is spoken mainly in the central region of the country and it is the first dialect of around 4.05 million people.

There are three major dialects of Najdi Arabic. There is Northern Najdi, spoken in Ha'il Region and Al-Qassim Region in the Najd; Central Najdi (Urban Najdi), spoken in the city of Riyadh and surrounding towns and farming communities; and Southern Najdi, spoken in the city of Al-Kharj and surrounding towns, and in the Rub' al-Khali.

In 1994, Bruce Ingham wrote of the region of Najd in Central Arabia that it had always been regarded as "inaccessible, ringed by a belt of sand deserts, the Nafud, Dahana and the Rub' al-Khali and often with its population at odds with the rulers of the outer settled lands. It is, however, the center of a purely Arabian culture based on a partnership between bedouin camel husbandry and settled palm cultivation. Possibly as a result of overpopulation, the bedouin have periodically spread over into the lands of the Fertile Crescent. Because of their isolated position, the Najdi dialect is of a very interesting and archaic type."

ARABIC PRONUNCIATIONS

PLEASE MASTER THE FOLLOWING PAGE IN ARABIC PRONUNCIATIONS PRIOR TO STARTING THE PROGRAM

Kha. For Middle Eastern languages including Arabic, Hebrew, Farsi, Pashto, Urdu, Hindi, etc., and also German, to properly pronounce the kh or ch is essential, for example, *Khaled* (a Muslim name) or *Chanukah* (a Jewish holiday) or *Nacht* ("night" in German). The best way to describe kh or ch is to say "ka" or "ha" while at the same time putting your tongue at the back of your throat and blowing air. It's pronounced similarly to the sound that you make when clearing your throat. Please remember this whenever you come across any word containing a kh in this program.

Ghayin. The Arabic gh is equivalent to the "g" in English, but its pronunciation more closely resembles the French "r," rather than "g." Pronounce it at the back of your throat. The sound is equivalent to what you would make when gargling water. Gha is pronounced more as "rha," rather than as "ga." *Ghada* is pronounced as "rhada." In this program, the symbol for *ghayin* is gh, so keep your eyes peeled.

Aayin is pronounced as a'a, pronounced deep at the back of your throat. Rather similar to the sound one would make when gagging. In the program, the symbol for *aayin* is a'a, u'u, o'o, or i'i.

Ha is pronounced as "ha." Pronunciation takes place deep at the back of your throat, and for correct pronunciation, one must constrict the back of the throat and exhale air while simultaneously saying "ha." In the program, this strong h ("ha") is emphasized whenever *ha, ah, hi, he,* or *hu* is encountered. In this program "7" will be occasionally used to signify *ha.*

NOTE TO THE READER

The purpose of this book is merely to enable you to communicate in the Najdi Arabic dialect. In the program itself (pages 17-38) you may notice that the composition of some of those sentences might sound rather clumsy. This is intentional. These sentences were formulated in a specific way to serve two purposes: to facilitate the easy memorization of the vocabulary and to teach you how to combine the words in order to form your own sentences for quick and easy communication, rather than making complete literal sense in the English language. So keep in mind that this is not a phrase book!

As the title suggests, the sole purpose of this program is for conversational use only. It is based on the mirror translation technique. These sentences, as well as the translations are not incorrect, just a little clumsy. Latin languages, Semitic languages, and Anglo-Germanic languages, as well as a few others, are compatible with the mirror translation technique.

Many users say that this method surpasses any other known language learning technique that is currently out there on the market. Just stick with the program and you will achieve wonders!

Again, I wish to stress this program is by no means, shape, or form a phrase book! The sole purpose of this book is to give you a fundamental platform to enable you to connect certain words to become conversational. Please also read the "Introduction" and the "About Me" section prior to commencing the program.

In order to succeed with my method, please start on the very first page of the program and fully master one page at a time prior to proceeding to the next. Otherwise, you will overwhelm yourself and fail. Please do not skip pages, nor start from the middle of the book.

It is a myth that certain people are born with the talent to learn a language, and this book disproves that myth. With this method, anyone can learn a foreign language as long as he or she follows these explicit directions:

* Memorize the vocabulary on each page

* Follow that memorization by using a notecard to cover the words you have just memorized and test yourself.

* Then read the sentences following that are created from the vocabulary bank that you just mastered.

* Once fully memorized, give yourself the green light to proceed to the next page.

Again, if you proceed to the following page without mastering the previous, you are guaranteed to gain nothing from this book. If you follow the prescribed steps, you will realize just how effective and simplistic this method is.

The Program

Let's Begin! "Vocabulary" (Memorize the Vocabulary)

I | I am - Ana
With you – Ana ma'ak
With him / with her - Ma'aah / Ma'aha
With us - Ma'ana
For you – Lek, ashanek
Without him – Bdonh
Without them – Bdonhom
Always - Dayim
Was – Kan
This, this is, it's, it is – (M) Hatha, Hatha ho **(F)** Hathy, Hathy he
Sometimes – Ahyanan
Maybe – Yimken
You / you are / are you – (M) Ant (F) Anty
You (plural) – Antoum
Is it - (M) Wessho, (F) Wesshy
Today – Elyoum
Better – Azyan / Ahsan
He / he is - Ho
She / she is - Hee
From - Min

This is for you
Hatha lek
I am from Saudi
Ana min Asu'udiayh
Are you from Riyadh?
Ant min e-Riyadh?
I am with you
Ana ma'ak
Sometimes you are with us at the mall
Ayanan ant ma'ana bl mall
I am always with her
Ana dayim ma'aha
Are you without them today?
Ant bdonhom elyoum?
Sometimes I am with him
Ahyanan ana ma'ah

*In Saudi Najdi Arabic, with the question "is it?", the "it" can pertain to either a masculine or feminine noun. However, whenever pertaining to a masculine or feminine noun, it will become *ho* or *he*. For example, when referring to a feminine noun such as *saiyarah* ("the car), "is it (the car in question) here?" / *he hena?* When referring to a masculine noun such as *kalb* ("a dog), "is it (the dog in question) on the table?" *ho 'ala etawlah?* However, I yet again wish to stress that this isn't a grammar book!

Ashanek is usually used in the context of doing something for someone. For example, "I'm doing that for you" is *ashanek*. However, *lek* is used when giving something to someone.

I was - Ana kent
To be - (**M**) Yekoon/ (**F**) Tkoon
The - Al /A
Same – Nafs
Good - Zēn
Here - Hena
Very – Marrah
And - W
Between – Bēn
Now – Elheen
Later / After / afterwards - Ba'ad / Ba'den
If - Etha
Yes – Ēh
To – Le
Tomorrow – Bokrah
You - (M) Ant / (F) Anty
Also / too / as well – Ba'ad
With them – Ma'ahom

If it's between now and later
Etha hatha bēn elheen w ba'den
It's better tomorrow
Ahsan bokrah
This is good as well
Hatha zēn ba'ad
To be the same person
Yekoon nafs ashakhs ashakhs
Yes, you are very good
Ēh, Ant marrah zēn
I was here with them
Ana knt hena ma'ahom
You and I
Ant w ana
The same day
Nafs elyoum

Me – (read footnote)
Ok – Taib
Even if - Hatta law
No – lla
Worse – Aswa'
Where – Wēn
Everything – Kel Shai
Somewhere – B mkan (ay makan means "anywhere")
What – Wessho?
Almost – Taqriban
There - Henak

Afterwards is worse
Ba'aden Aswa'
Even if I go now
Hatta law arooh elheen
Where is everything?
Wēn kel shai
Maybe somewhere
Yimken b makan
What? I am almost there
Wessho? Ana taqriban henak
Where are you?
Ant wēn / Anty wēn
Where is the airport?
Wēn elmataar?

*" There" has two meanings, *fe* or *hnak* depending on the context, when we say there is we say *fe* / but when we say "I am there (place)" we say *ana hnak*.

*In Arabic, the pronoun "me" has several definitions. In relation to verbs, it's *le*. Le refers to any verb that relates to the action of doing something to someone or for someone.
For example, "tell me," "tell (to) me" / *(M) gool le*.
'ni' just means "me": "love me" / *hebbeni*
Other variations (*e,i*):
  * "on me" / *'alai*, "in me" / *fe*, "to me" / *le*, "with me" / *ma'ai*
The same rule applies for "him" and "her"—both become suffixes: *–o* and *–a*.
Basically all verbs pertinent to male end with *h*, and all pertinent to female end with *ha*.
  * "love her" / *ahebha*
  * "love him" / *ahebbah*
  * "love them" / *ahebhom*
  * "love us" / *ahebbena*
Any verb that relates to doing someone to someone, for someone put *l*:
  * "tell her" / *gool laha*
  * "tell him" / *gool lah*
  * "tell them" / *gool lhom*
  * "tell us" / *gool lena*
Adding you as a suffix in Arabic is *ek* or *lek*. *(both masc and fem are the same)*
  * "love you" / *ahebbek*
  * "tell you" / *agool lek*

House – Bēt
In / at - Fe / Be
Car – Saiyarah
Already – Aslan
Good morning - Sabah el kheir
How are you? – Shlonek?
Where are you from? – (M) Min wēn ant? (F) Min wēn anty?
Today – Elyoum
Hello – Hala
What is your name? – Shesmek?
How old are you? - Kam omrek?
Son – Walad
Daughter – Bent
To have – (M) 'Endah/ (F) 'Endeha
Doesn't – Ma / La
Hard – Sa'ab
Still – Baqi
Then (or "so") – Ba'den / Taib ("Then" can be "Ba'den" like "next", but when "then" is like "so" so it will be "Taib" so choose the context you want)
In order to – 'Ashan

She doesn't have a car, so maybe she is still at the house?
Hee ma 'endeha saiyarah, yemkin hee baqi belbait?
I am in the car already with your son and daughter
Ana be saiyarah aslan ma'a wldek w bntek
Good morning, how are you today?
Sabah el kheir, shlonek elyoum?
Hello, what is your name?
Hala, Shesmek?
How old are you?
Kam omrek?
This is very hard, but it's not impossible
Hatha sa'ab marrah, bas mub mustaheel
Then where are you from?
Taib Min wēn Ant?

*In Arabic, possessive pronouns become suffixes to the noun. For example, in the translation for "your," ek. (again, both are the same)
- "your book" / *ktabek*, "your house" / *bētek*
*In Saudi Arabic *a* is used to indicate cases of "to" or "to be able to." You will notice in the program *ka* will quite often become a prefix to the verb "I want to learn," *ana abe at'alam* or "in order to be able to go" *agdar arooh*.

Thank you –Shukran
For – 'Ashan
Anything - Ay shai
That / That is – (F) Hathik / (M) Hathak
Time – Wagt (duration) / Sa'a (if asking about the clock)
But - Bas
No / not - La / Mu / Mub
I am not - Ana ma / ana mu / ana mub
Away - B'eed
Late – Meta'kher
Similar – Methl / Zay/ m
Another/ other – Thany / Ghēr
Side – Jamb
Until – Elen/len
Yesterday – Elbareh / Ams
Without us – Bedonna
Since – Min lamma
Day - Youm
Before – Gabl

Thanks for everything
Shukran ala kel shai
It's almost time
Hatha alwagt tagreban
I am not here, I am away
Ana mub hena, ana b'eed
That is a similar house
Hatha methl elbēt
I am from the other side
Ana min makan thany
But I was here until late yesterday
Bas ana knt hena len taly ellail ams
I am not at the other house
Ana mu be elbēt elthany

*In Saudi Arabic regarding negations, such as "no", "not", "doesn't", "can't", "don't" it's either *ma* or *mu* or *la*. *La* is used to indicate cases such as "are you here?" *ant hena?* then you reply "no" *la*. *Mu* is used to indicate cases of "not," "doesn't," "don't," for example: "I am not at the other house" is *ana mu fi elbait el ethani*. In some instances both cases of *la* and *ma* may be used, for example; "can you come?" "No I can't" *la ma aqdar*.

*In Saudi Arabic, there are three definitions for time:
- "time" / *mudda* refers to "era", "moment period," "duration of time."
- "time(s)" / *marrah(t)* / wagt *(t)* refers to "occasion" or "frequency."
- "time" / *sa'ah* references "hour," "what time is it?"

*This isn't a phrase book! The purpose of this book is solely to provide you with the tools to create your own sentences!

What time is it? – Kam a-sa'aa?
I say / I am saying – Agool
I want - Ana abe / abe
Without you – Bdoonek
Everywhere /wherever – Kel makan
I go – Barooh
With - Ma'
My – Le
Cousin (paternal) - (M) Walad
'ammy / (F) Bent 'ammy / (P) (M)
'Eiyal 'ammy / (P)(F) Banaat 'ammy
Cousin (maternal) - (M) Walad khaly
/ (F) Bent khali / (P)(M) 'Eiyal khaly
/ (P)(F) Banaat khaly
I need – Ahtaj
Right now – Elheen
Night – Lēl
To see – Yeshoof
Light - Noor
Outside – Barra
Without – Bdoon
Happy – Farhan / Mistans
I see / I am seeing – Ashoof
I am saying no / I say no - Agool la

I want to see this today
Abe ashoof hatha elyoum
I am with you everywhere
Ana ma'ak b kel makan
I am happy without my cousins here
Ana mistans bedoon walad 'ammy hena
I need to be there at night
Ahtaj akoon hnak be elēl
I see light outside
Ashoof noor barra
What time is it right now?
Kam elsa'ah elheen?

*"Mine" / *haggi* is also a possessive pronoun. *Haggi* means "my" but also becomes a suffix to a noun. Nouns ending in a vowel end with *–the*. Nouns ending with a consonant end with *–eh*. For example:
   * "cousin" / *iben el 'amm*, "my cousin" / *iben 'ammy*
   * "cup" / *cob*, "my cup" / *cobi*
For second and third person masculine noun, *walad* ("son"), (S) *ek*, (P) *kom*)
   * "your son" / *waladk*, "your (plural) son" / *waladkom*
   * "his son" / *waladh*, "her son" / *waladha*
   * "our son" / *waladna*
   * "their son" / *waladhom*
For second and third person feminine noun: "car" / *saiyarah*
   * "your car" / *saiyartek*, "your (plural) car" / *saiyartkom*
   * "his car" / *saiyarteh*, "her car" / *saiyaratha*
   * "our car" / *saiyaratna*
   * "their car" / *saiyarathom*

Place – Makan
Easy - Sahel
To find - Yelga / Telga
To look for / to search – Yedawwer
Near / Close - Gereeb
To wait – Yehtery / yentedher
To sell - (M) Ybee' - (F) tbee'
To use – Yesta'amel
To know – Ye'ref
To decide – Yqarrir
Between - Bēn
Both – Thnēn/ Kelehom
To – 'Ashan (preceding a verb)

This place it's easy to find
Hatha almkan sahel algah
I want to look for this next to the car
Ana abe ashoof jamb asaiyarah
I am saying to wait until tomorrow
Ana agool nentedher len bokrah
This table is easy to sell
Hathi atawlah sahel tenba'
I want to use this
Abe asta'mel hathi
I need to know where is the house
Ahtaj a'aref wēn elbēt
I want to decide between both places
Abe aqarrer bēn almkanen

Because – 'Ashan
To buy – Ashtry
They - Hom
Them | Their – Hom
Bottle - Qarorah
Book - Ktab
Mine - Haggi
To understand – Yefham
Problem / Problems - (S) Mushkilah
I do / I am doing - Assawi
Of - Min
To look – Yshoof
Myself - Nafsi
Enough – Khalas / Yekkafi
Food / water - Akil / Moya
Each/ every/ entire/ all – Kl
Hotel - Fondoq

I like this hotel because I want to look at the beach
Ajbni hatha alfondoq ashan weddi ashoof alshate'
I want to buy a bottle of water
Ana abe ashtry qarorat moya
I do this everyday
Ana asswai ketha kl youm
Both of them have enough food
Ethnenhom endhom akl yekkafi
That is the book, and that book is mine
Hatha elktab, w hatha elktab haggi
I need to understand the problem
Ana ahtaj afham almushkilah
I see the view of the city from the hotel
Ashoof mandhar almadinah min alfondoq
I do my homework today
Asswai wajbati alyoum
My entire life (*all my life* **)**
Kl hayati / kl omri

*"Both of them" is *ethnen*.

24

I like – Ye'jbni/ Aheb
There is / There are – Fe
Family / Parents - 'Aylah / Waldēn / Ahel
Why – Lēsh
To say – Ygool
Something – Hajah / Shai
To go – Namshy / (M) Yimshy / (F) Timshy
Ready – Jahiz
Soon - Qereeb
To work – Ashteghil / (M) Yeshteghil / (F) Teshteghil
Who – Min
To know – A'aref
That (conjunction) **–** Enha

I like to be at my house with my parents
Ye'ajbni akon bilbēt ma' ahle
I want to know why I need to say something important
Ana weddi a'aref lēsh ana ahtaj agool shai mohem
I am there with him
Ana hnak ma'ah
I am busy, but I need to be ready soon
Ana mashghool, bass ahtaj akon jahiz gereeb
I like to go to work
Aheb arooh alshghl
'Who is there?
Min hnak?
I want to know if they are here, because I want to go outside
Ana abe a'aref etha hom hena, ashan abe arooh barra / weddi atla'a
There are seven dolls
Fee sab'e al'aab
I need to know that it is a good idea
Ahtaj a'aref enha hatha fekrah zēnah

*In the last sentence, we use "that" as a conjunction (*enha*) and a demonstrative pronoun (M) *hatha* (F) *hatha'he*.

25

How much /how many – Kam
To bring – Ajeeb
With me – Ma'ai
Instead - Badal
Only – Bass / Lamma
When – Mita
Or – Aw
I can / Can I – Ana agdar / Agdar ana
Were - Kano
Without me - Bedooni
Fast – Bser'aah
Slow – Shway / B-shwaysh
Cold – Bard
Inside – Jowwa / Dakhel
To eat – Yakil
Hot – Haar
To Drive – Ysooq

How much money do I need to bring with me?
Kam floos ajeeb ma'ai?
Instead of this cake, I want that cake
Badal hatha al cake, abe hatha al cake
Only when you can
Bas lamma tegder
They were without me yesterday
Hom kano bdooni ams
Do I need to drive the car fast or slow?
Ahtaj asooq esaiyarah bser'aah wala bshwaysh?
It is cold inside the library
Bard dakhel el-maktabeh
Yes, I like to eat this hot for my lunch
Eē, aheb akil haar bil-ghada
I can work today
Agdar asht'eghel alyoum

*"Were" is *kano*, but for "they were," "We were" is *kenna*.
*"I can" and "can I?" is *ana agdar*. "You can" or "can you?" is *Ant tegdr?*

To answer – Yerred (to respond) / Yejaweb (to answer a question)
To fly – Yeteer / Yesafer
Time / Times - Marrah / Marrat
To travel – Yesafer
To learn - (M) Yt'allam / (F) Tet'allam
How - Kēf
To swim - (M) Yesbah / (F) Tesbah
To practice – Yetmarran
To play - Yel'aab
To leave – Yerooh / Yetla'a /
Many /much /a lot - Ktheer
I go to – Arooh le
First – L'awl
Time / Times – Marrah / Marrat

I want to answer many questions
Ana abe ajwaeb as'ilah ktheerah
I must fly to Dubai today
Ana lazim asafer Dubai elyoum
I need to learn how to swim at the pool
Ana ahtaj at'allam kif asbah bil masbah
I want to learn to play better tennis
Abe at'allam al'aab tennis ahsan
I want to leave this here for you when I go to travel the world
Abe akhalli hatha hena lk lamma arooh asafer el 'aalamm
Since the first time
Min awal marrah
The children are yours
Elbezran lek

*In Saudi Najdi dialect, "to leave (something)" is *ykhalli*. "To leave (a place)" is *yikhrej*.
*In Najdi dialect, there are three definitions for time:
    - "time" / *mudda* refers to "era", "moment period," "duration of time."
    - "time(s)" / *marra(t)* refers to "occasion" or "frequency."
    - "time" / *sa'ah* references "hour," "what time is it?"
With the knowledge you've gained so far, now try to create your own sentences!

Nobody / anyone – Mahad / Ay ahad

Against - Dhed

Us – Ehna/ Henna

To visit - Yzoor

Mom / Mother – Ommi / Yummah

To give – Ye'ty

Which – Ay

To meet – Yegabel/ Yeshoof

Someone – Ahad

Just - Bass

To walk - Ytmasha

Around – Hawalin

Towards – Gurb

Than - Min

Nothing – Abad / Mafe shai / Wala shai

Something is better than nothing
Shai ahsan min wala shai

I am against him
Ana dheddeh

Is there anyone here?
Fe ahad hena?

We go to visit my family each week
Henna nzoor el ahil kl asboo'

I need to give you something
Ahtaj a'ateek shai

Do you want to go meet someone?
Tabe tgabel ahad?

I was here on Wednesdays as well
Ana kent hena el arba' ba'ad

Do you do every day
Ent tssawai hatha kl youm?

You need to walk around, but not towards the house
Ant tehtaj tmshy, bass mub gurb elbēt

*In Arabic, when using the pronoun "you" as a direct and indirect object pronoun (the person who is actually affected by the action that is being carried out) in relation to a verb, the pronoun "you" becomes a suffix to that verb. That suffix becomes *ek*.

* "to give" / *a'te* "to give you" / *a'teek*
* "to tell" / *qool* "to tell you" / *qoolek*
* "see you" / *ashoofek*: "to see you" (plural) / *ashoofkom*

For third person male, add *oh* and *hom* for plural, for female add h*a* and h*on* for plural.

* "tell him" / *qoolo*
* "tell her" / *qool-lha*
* "see them" / *shoofhom*
* "see us "/ *shoofena*

I have – 'Endy
Don't - La
Friend – Sedeeg
To borrow – Ytsallaf
To look like / resemble – Yeshbah
Like (preposition) – Zai/ Methel
Grandfather – Jad
To want - Yabe
To stay – Yjles / Yeq'ed
To continue – Ekammel
Way – Tereeq
I don't - Ana ma rah
To show - Yewarry
To prepare – Yejjahez
I am not going – Ana mub raih

Do you want to look like Salim
Tabe tseer teshabah Salim
I want to borrow this book for my grandfather
Abe atsalaf hatha el ktab l-jaddy
I want to drive and to continue on this way to my house
Abe asooq w akamel 'ala hathak etereeq l-bēt'ee
I have a friend there, that's why I want to stay in Riyadh
'endy sedeegi henak, ashan ketha weddi agles be-Riyadh
I am not going to see anyone here
Ana ma rah ashoof ahad hena
I need to show you how to prepare breakfast
Ahtaj awareek kēf tssawi elfotoor
Why don't you have the book?
Lēsh ma ma'ak el-ktab?
That is incorrect, I don't need the car today
Hatha ghalat, ana ma ahtaj esaiyarah elyoum

*In Saudi Arabic the case of "you don't have" is *ma e'ndek* or *ma ma'ak* or *ma 'endy*.

To remember - Ytthakkar
Your - Tek
Number - Raqm
Hour - Sa'aa
Dark / darkness – Dhalam
About / on the - 'Ala
Grandmother - Jadda / my grandmother - Jaddety
Five - Khams
Minute / minutes - Dqeeqa / Dqayq
More – Akthar
To think – Yfakker
To do – Yessawi
To come – Yejy
To hear - Ysma'
Last – Akheer / Akher

You need to remember my number
Tehtaj tet'thakkar raqmy
This is the last hour of darkness
Hathy akher Sa'aa min alēl/ adhalam
I want to come and to hear my grandmother speak Saudi Arabic
Abe ajy w Asma' jaddety tetkalm 'araby Saudi
I need to think more about this, and what to do
Ahtaj afakker fe hatha akthar, w wesh assawi
From here to there, it's only five minutes
Min hena len henak, bass khams dqayq
The school on the mountain
Elmadresah ala al jabal

To leave – Nkhrej / Netla'
Again – Ba'ad
Arabic - Arabi
To take - Nakheth
To try – Ajreb / Ahawel
To rent – A'ajer
Without her - Bedonha
We are – Henna
To turn off - Ytaffy
To ask – Ys'al
To stop - Ywqqf
Permission – Ethn

He needs to leave and rent a house at the beach
Ho yhtaj ykhrej w y'ajer bēt ala e shate'e
I want to take the test without her
Abe akheth el emtehan bedonha
We are here a long time
Henna hena min wagt toweel
I need to turn off the lights early tonight
Ahtaj ataffy enoor badry elyoum
We want to stop here
Nabe nwgef hena
We are from Al-Qassim
Henna min e-qassim
The same building
Nafs elemarah / elmabna
I want to ask permission to leave
Ana abe ethn ashan atla'
I want to sleep
Ana abe anam

To open - Yeftah
A bit, a little, a little bit - Shway
To pay – Yedfa'
Once again – Marrah thanyah
There isn't/ there aren't - Mafi
Sister - Ekht
To hope – Atmna
To live - Y'eesh
Nice to meet you – Tsharafna
Name - Esm
Last name – Esm el 'ayla
To return – Yerja'
Door - Baab

I need to open the door for my sister
Ana ahtaj aftah elbaab l-ekhty
I need to buy something
Ana ahtaj ashtry shai
I want to meet your sisters
Ana abe agabil khawatek
Nice to meet you, what is your name and your last name
Tsharafna, shesmek w shesm 'ayltek?
To hope for a little better
Yetmana shai ahsan shway
I want to return from the United States and to live in Qatar without problems
Ana abe arja' min Amrika w a'eesh b Qatar bedon mashakel
Why are you sad right now?
Lēsh za'alan elheen?
There aren't any people here
Mafi nas hena
There isn't enough time to go to Al-Kharj today
Mafi waqt yakkafi nrooh lel kharj el-youm

*In Saudi Arabic, regarding the verb "to meet" there are two separate cases to define this verb; *tgabil.* Depending of the context: to meet for business is *agabil* like in the sentence "do you want to go meet someone?" However, for meeting the sister, is getting acquainted with her, here it's *'tgabil.*
*This *isn't* a phrase book! The purpose of this book is *solely* to provide you with the tools to create *your own* sentences!

To happen – Yeseer
To order – Yetleb
To drink -Yeshrab
Excuse me - (M) Law smaht / (F) Law smahati
Child - (M) Walad (**F**) Bint
Woman – Marah
To begin / to start - Ybda
To finish – Yekhales
To help – Yesa'ed
To smoke - Yedakhen
To love - Yheb
To talk / to speak – Ytkallam

This must happen today
Hatha lazim yeseer el-youm
Excuse me, my child is here as well
Law smaht, weldi hena ba'ad
I love you
Ana ahebek
I see you
Ana ashoofek
I need you at my side
Ahtajak jambi
I need to begin soon to be able to finish at 3 o'clock in the afternoon
Ahtaj abda badri ashan agdar akhalles ala essa'a 3 aldhuhr
I need help
Ahtaj mosa'adah
I don't want to smoke once again
Ana ma abe adakhen marrah thanya
I want to learn how to speak Arabic
Abe at'allam kēf atkallam arabi

*"To be able to" is *agdar-word- ex. To be able to learn - agdar at'allam.*

To read - Yeqra
To write - Yekteb
To teach – Y'allem
To close - Yeqfel
To choose - Yekhtar
To prefer - Yefaddell
To put - Yehett
Less - Agal
Sun - Shamss
Month - Shahr
I talk - Atkallam
Exact – Madhboot

I need this book to learn how to read and write in Arabic because I want to teach in Egypt
Ahtaj hatha el-ktaab ashan at'allam kēf agra w aktb bel 'arabi ashan abe a'allem b maser
I want to close the door of the house
Abe aqafel baab elbēt
I prefer to put the gift here
Afaddell ahett el hadeyah hena
I want to pay less than you for the dinner
Abe adfaa' agal minnek lel-'asha
I speak with the boy and the girl in French
Ana atkallam ma' elwlad w elbent bl faransi
There is sun outside today
Fe shamss barra el-youm
Is it possible to know the exact date?
Tegder te'aref alwaqt elmadhboot?

*"For the" is *lel*
*"In" is *bl*
With the knowledge you've gained so far, now try to create your own sentences!

34

To exchange (money**)** – Yebadel (m)/ Tbadel (f)
To call – Yenade
Brother – Ukho
Dad – Ubo
To sit - Yejles
Together – Sawa / Ma' ba'adh
To change – Yeghayyer
Of course - Akeed
Welcome – Hala
During – Youm
Years - (**S**)'Aam / Sana / (**P**) 'A'waam / Senen
Sky - Sama
Up – Foq
Down - Taht
Sorry - Aseff
To follow - Yelhag
To the - Le
Big - Kbir
New - Jdeed
Never / ever - 'Omry ma / Abad

I don't want to exchange this money at the bank
Ana ma abe abadel el floos bl-bank
I want to call my brother and my dad today
Ana abe akallim ukhoy w uboy el-youm
Of course I can come to the theater, and I want to sit together with you and with your sister
Akeed agdar aje lel massrah, w ana abe njles sawa ma'ak w ma' ekhtek
I need to go down to see your new house
Abe arooh ashoof bētek el jdeed
I can see the sky from the window
Agdar ashoof elsama min elshibbak
I am sorry, but he wants to follow her to the store
Ana aseff, bass ho yabi yelhgha lelmahal
I don't ever want to see you again
Ma abe ashoofek marrah thanyah

*In Saudi Najdi dialect, brother is *ukho,* and dad is *ubo*. However, "my dad" is *ubooy* and "my brother" is *ukhoy*. "My sister" is *ekhtey*, and "my mother" is *ommi*.
*For the possessive pronouns, her (*ha*) and him (*eh*), both become suffixes to the verb or noun. Concerning nouns: her house / *bētha*, his house / *bēteh*.

To allow - Yesmah
To believe – Yesaddeg
Morning – Sbaah
Except - Ma 'ada / Ella
To promise - Yw'ed
Good night – Tesbah ala khair
To recognize - Ye'araf
People - Naas
To move - Yharrek
Far - B'eed
Different – ghēr
Man - rajjal
To enter - Yedkhel
To receive – Yestagbil
Throughout – Min bēn
Good evening – Masa alkheir
Left / right - Ysar / Yemeen

I need to allow him to go with us, he is a different man now
Ahtaj akhallih yeji m'aana, ho rajjal ghēr alheen
I believe everything except this
Ana asaddeg kl shai ella hatha
I promise to say good night to my parents each night
Wa'ad eni agol tesbah ala khair le ahli kl lēlah
The people from Jordan are very pleasant
Enas min elordon hlēleen
I need to find another hotel very quickly
Ahtaj alga fondog thany bsr'aa
They need to receive a book for work
Hom yehtajon yakhthon kitaab le shegel
I see the sun in the morning
Ana ashoof elshams b-sabah
The house is on the right side of the street
Elbēt ala eljamb elyemeen min elshare'

To wish - Atmanna
Bad – Shēn
To get - Akheth
To forget - Ansa
Everybody / Everyone - Kl wahed
Although – Ma' in
To feel - Ahiss
Great – Zēn
Next (as in close, near) - Jamb
Next (as in next year) - Jai
To like – Yej'eb
In front – Qeddam
Person - Shakhs
Behind – Wara
Well – Ahsan
Restaurant – Mata'am
Bathroom – Hammam
Goodbye – Ma' alsalama

I don't want to wish you anything bad
Ana ma atmana lek ay shai shēn
I must forget everybody from my past to feel well
Ana lazim ansa kl wahed min el madhy ashan aseer ahsan.
I am next to the person behind you
Ana jamb el shakhs elly warak
There is a great person in front of me
Fe wahed zēn qeddami.
I say goodbye to my friends
Ana aqool ma' alsalama l asdega'e
Where is the bathroom in the restaurant?
Wēn alhammam bl mata'am?
She has to get a car before the next year
He lazim takheth saiyarah qabl esana el jaiah
I like the house, but it is very small
Ajbni elbēt, bass marrah segheer

Jamb literally means "side." In Arabic, it refers to "next." *jamb* is "besides me" and *jambek* is "besides you."

To remove / to take out - Yeshel
Please - Tekfa
Beautiful - (**M**)Mazyoon/Helo (**F**) Mazyoonah /Helwah
To lift – Yerfa'
Include / Including - Yeshmal
Belong – Yantami le/ mub min
To hold - Yemsak
To check – Yeraje' / Yeta'akad
Small - Segheer
Real - Sedgi
Week – Esboo'
Size – Hajm / Magas
Even though – Hatta law
Doesn't – Ma
So (as in "then") **–** Ya'ny / W baa'den
So (as in "so big") **–** Marrah
Price – Se'er

She wants to remove this door please
He tabe tsheel elbab law smaht
This doesn't belong here, I need to check again
Hatha mub min hena, ahtaj at'akad marrah thanyah
This week the weather was very beautiful
Hatha El esboo' aljaw marrah helo
I need to know which is the real diamond
Ahtaj a'aref ay almasa hqeeqya
We need to check the size of the house
Nehtaj neshoof hajm elbēt
I want to lift this, so you need to hold it high
Abe asheel hatha, ya'ny lazim temsakah foq
I can pay this even though that the price is expensive
Agdar adfa' hatha hatta law else'er ghali
Including everything is this price correct?
Shamel kl shai hatha alse'er sah?

Countries of the Middle East
Bilad al-sharq al- awsatt

Lebanon - Lobnan
Syria - Surya
Jordan - L-ordon
Saudi Arabia - Asu'udiayh
Israel /Palestine /West Bank -
Isra'eel / Felesteen / el-deffah
algharbiyyah
Bahrain - l-Bahrein
Yemen - l-Yaman
Oman - 'Oman
United Arab Emirates - l-Emarat
el'arabyah el-metahedah
Kuwait - l-Kwait
Iraq - l-Iraq
Qatar - Qatar
Morocco - el-maghreb
Algeria - l-Jazayer
Libya - Leebya
Egypt - Maser
Tunisia - Tunes

Months
January - Ynayr
February - Febrayr
March – Mares
April - Ebreel
May - May
June – June
July - July
August - Aughustus
September – September
October - Oktobar
November - November
December - December

Days of the Week
Sunday - El- ahad
Monday - El-aethnen
Tuesday - El-tholatha
Wednesday - El-arbe'aa
Thursday - El-khamees
Friday - Jem'aah
Saturday - Sabt

Seasons
Spring – Rabee'
Summer - Sēf
Autumn - Khareef
Winter - Shetta

Cardinal Directions
North - Shamaal
South - Janoob
East – Sharq
West - Gharb

Colors

Black - Aswad
White - Abyadh
Gray - Rmadi
Red - Ahamr
Blue - Azraq
Yellow - Asfar
Green - Akhdhar
Orange – Brtgali
Purple - Banfsaji
Brown - Bunni

Numbers

One - Wahed
Two - Thnen
Three – Thlath
Four - Arb'aa
Five - Khams
Six - Sitt
Seven - Sab'a
Eight - Thman
Nine – Tis'a
Ten - 'Ashr
Twenty/ Thirty - 'Eshreen /Thalatheen
Hundred - Miyyah
Thousand – Alf
Million – Malyoon

Conversational
Arabic Quick
and Easy

SAUDI (Hijazi) DIALECT

YATIR NITZANY

THE SAUDI HIJAZI DIALECT

Like every other Middle Eastern nation, the official language of Saudi Arabia is Modern Standard Arabic, which is taught as a second language to most citizens of the country. Each country may have its own dialects, but MSA unifies them all and helps them communicate with each other almost flawlessly. Saudi Arabia houses three dialects; these are the mother tongues for most citizens. The main one is Najdi, which is spoken in central Saudi Arabia and is the first language of almost one-third of the country. It is considered an upper-class dialect; for example, the royal family speaks this language.

Another dialect in Saudi Arabia is Gulf Arabic, which is also called Shargi. Shargi is found mostly in the eastern areas of the country.

The third dialect, and the one described in this book, is Hijazi Arabic or Hijazi Arabic, which is spoken in the western area of Saudi Arabia. Hijazi Arabic, also known as West Arabian Arabic, is the most common and popular dialect in the Saudi Peninsula. It is spoken along the coast of the Red Sea, especially in the cities of Mecca and Jeddah, and is also used as the main means of communication. For example, much of the Saudi Arabian life is conveyed with this dialect in regards to trade and government. North Hijazi has four sub-varieties, and South Hijazi has sixteen.

While there are two main groups of dialects spoken in the Hejaz region – the urban population who consist the majority, and the Bedouin rural population – the term most often applies to the urban variety, spoken in the major cities such as Jeddah, Mecca, Medina, Ta'if, and Yanbu.

Spoken in: Western Saudi Arabia

ARABIC PRONUNCIATIONS

PLEASE MASTER THE FOLLOWING PAGE IN ARABIC PRONUNCIATIONS PRIOR TO STARTING THE PROGRAM

Kha. For Middle Eastern languages including Arabic, Hebrew, Farsi, Pashto, Urdu, Hindi, etc., and also German, to properly pronounce the kh or ch is essential, for example, *Khaled* (a Muslim name) or *Chanukah* (a Jewish holiday) or *Nacht* ("night" in German). The best way to describe kh or ch is to say "ka" or "ha" while at the same time putting your tongue at the back of your throat and blowing air. It's pronounced similarly to the sound that you make when clearing your throat. Please remember this whenever you come across any word containing a kh in this program.

Ghayin. The Arabic gh is equivalent to the "g" in English, but its pronunciation more closely resembles the French "r," rather than "g." Pronounce it at the back of your throat. The sound is equivalent to what you would make when gargling water. Gha is pronounced more as "rha," rather than as "ga." *Ghada* is pronounced as "rhada." In this program, the symbol for *ghayin* is gh, so keep your eyes peeled.

Aayin is pronounced as a'a, pronounced deep at the back of your throat. Rather similar to the sound one would make when gagging. In the program, the symbol for *aayin* is *a'a, u'u, o'o,* or *i'i.*

Ha is pronounced as "ha." Pronunciation takes place deep at the back of your throat, and for correct pronunciation, one must constrict the back of the throat and exhale air while simultaneously saying "ha." In the program, this strong h ("ha") is emphasized whenever *ha, ah, hi, he,* or *hu* is encountered.

NOTE TO THE READER

The purpose of this book is merely to enable you to communicate in the Saudi Hijazi Arabic dialect. In the program itself (pages 17-38) you may notice that the composition of some of those sentences might sound rather clumsy. This is intentional. These sentences were formulated in a specific way to serve two purposes: to facilitate the easy memorization of the vocabulary and to teach you how to combine the words in order to form your own sentences for quick and easy communication, rather than making complete literal sense in the English language. So keep in mind that this is not a phrase book!

As the title suggests, the sole purpose of this program is for conversational use only. It is based on the mirror translation technique. These sentences, as well as the translations are not incorrect, just a little clumsy. Latin languages, Semitic languages, and Anglo-Germanic languages, as well as a few others, are compatible with the mirror translation technique.

Many users say that this method surpasses any other known language learning technique that is currently out there on the market. Just stick with the program and you will achieve wonders!

Again, I wish to stress this program is by no means, shape, or form a phrase book! The sole purpose of this book is to give you a fundamental platform to enable you to connect certain words to become conversational. Please also read the "Introduction" and the "About Me" section prior to commencing the program.

In order to succeed with my method, please start on the very first page of the program and fully master one page at a time prior to proceeding to the next. Otherwise, you will overwhelm yourself and fail. Please do not skip pages, nor start from the middle of the book.

It is a myth that certain people are born with the talent to learn a language, and this book disproves that myth. With this method, anyone can learn a foreign language as long as he or she follows these explicit directions:

* Memorize the vocabulary on each page

* Follow that memorization by using a notecard to cover the words you have just memorized and test yourself.

* Then read the sentences following that are created from the vocabulary bank that you just mastered.

* Once fully memorized, give yourself the green light to proceed to the next page.

Again, if you proceed to the following page without mastering the previous, you are guaranteed to gain nothing from this book. If you follow the prescribed steps, you will realize just how effective and simplistic this method is.

The Program

Let's Begin! "Vocabulary" (Memorize the Vocabulary)

I | I am – Ana
With you – **(Masculine)** Ma'ak /
(Fem) ma'aky
With him /with her - Ma'ah/ma'aha
With us - Ma'ana
For you - **(M)** Ashanak/ **(F)** Ashanek
Without him – Men ghero/ men
Dono
Without them –Mengherahom/ mo
ma'ahom
Always –Daiman
Was – Kan
This, this is, it is – Daak/haad/
hade
Is, is it? – Haadak/ howa/ heye *(see
footnote below)*
Sometimes - Ahyanan / awgat
Maybe – Balken
You / you are / are you – **(M)** Enta
(F) enty
You (plural) - Entom
Better – Tamam / ahsan
He / he is –Howwa
She / she is –Heya
From - Min

This is for you
Hada Ashanak
I am from Saudi Arabia
Ana men a-sa'udia
Are you from Riyadh?
Enta men al reyad? / enty men al
reyad?
I am with you
Ana ma'ak
Sometimes you are with us at the mall
Ahyanan ente ma'ana fel mall
I am always with her
Ana daiman ma'aha
Are you without them today?
Enta/enty mo ma'ahom elyoum?
Sometimes I am with him
Ahyanan akoon ma'aah

* In Saudi Arabia, there are gender rules. Saying "for you" to a male is *'ashanak*, but if you are talking to a female, it's *'ashanek*. "This is for you" means it belongs to you and, hence, in this case we use *ashanak*. However, if the sentence was "I did it for you" (i.e., I did this only because you are a special friend to me or because you mean a lot to me), here in this context we use *sawet-ha luki* for the girl and *sawet-ha luk* for the boy.
* In Arabic with the question "is it?", the "it" can pertain to either a masculine or feminine noun. However, whenever pertaining to a masculine or feminine noun, it will become *howe*
Howa or *heya*. For example, when referring to a feminine noun such as *seyara* ("the car), "is it (the car in question) here?" / *heya hena?* When referring to a masculine noun such as *kalb* ("a dog), "is it (the dog in question) on the table?" *howe 'ala al ttawlah?* For neuter, it's *hadaak?* However, I yet again wish to stress that this isn't a grammar book!

I was – Ana kont
To be - (**M**) Yekoon/ (**F**)tekoon
The – Al
Same – Nafs / nafs ashshay
Good – Kwayes / tamaam
Here – Hena
Very – Ktheer / marra
And - Wa
Between – Ma ben
Now – Daheen
Later / after / afterwards – Ba'deen/ mo daheen
If – Law
Yes – Ewaa
To – Ela
Tomorrow - Bokra
Day - Youm
Also / too / as well – Kaman / esh tany

If it's between now and later
Law kan been daheen wa ba'deen
It's better tomorrow
Ahsan bokra
This is good as well
Hada tamaam kaman
To be the same person
Yekoon nafs ashshaks
Yes, you are very good
Eywa ente kways marra
I was here with them
Kont hena ma'ahom
You and I
Ente wa ana
The same day
Nafs elyoum

*In the Arabic language, adjectives usually proceed the noun. For example:
* "small house" / *bait sageer*
* "tall person" / *shakhs taweel*
* "short person" / *shakhs gaseer*

There are exceptions, though. For example, when expressing admiration or something impressive, we can say, "How big is this house?" / *da Al bait marra kabeer?*

Me - Ana

Ok – Aiwa

Even if – Hata law /law esh

No - La

Worse – Aswaa'

Where – Fain

Everything – Kol haja

Somewhere – Medry fain

What - Esh

Almost - Yo'tabar / tagreeban

There – Henaka

Afterwards is worse

Ba'deen aswaa'

Even if I go now

Hata law roht daheen

Where is everything?

Ween kol haga?

Maybe somewhere

Balken medry fain

What? I am almost there

Esh? Ana O'tabar (Tagreenan)

henaka **Where are you?**

(M)Enta/ (F) enty

*In Arabic, the pronoun "me" has several definitions. In relation to verbs its *anee /
lee*. *Lee* refers to any verb that relates to the action of doing something to someone
or for someone. For example, "tell me," "tell (to) me" / *(M) gool lee*

Ni just means "me": "love me" / *hobbany* or "see me" / *Shofany*

Other variations (*le, ne*):

* "on me" / *'alaya*, "in me" / *fia*
* "to me" / *ashani*, "with me" / *ma'aya*
* "in front of me" / *goddami*, "from me" / *meny*

The same rule applies for "him" and "her"; both become suffixes; *o* and *a*. Basically
all verbs pertinent to male end with O and all pertinent to female end with A).

* "love her" / *hobbaha*, "love him" / *hobbo*
* "love them" / *hobbahom*, "love us" / *hobbana*

Any verb that relates to doing something to someone, for someone put *l*:

* "tell her" / *goolaha*
* "tell him" / *golloh*
* "tell them" / *gollahom*
* "tell us" / *goolana*

Adding you as a suffix in Arabic is *ak* female *ek*

* "love you" / (M) *Ahebak* / (F) Ahebek
* "tell you" / *(M) agoolak* / (F) *agoolek*

*In Hijazi dialect, to signify "even if" we use either *law esh* or *hatta law*. *Law esh* is
used when you say "whatever happens." For example, "whatever happens, I
won't talk to him again," then you say *law esh hasal, ma rah atkallam m'ah mara thanya*.
However, "even if" / *hatta law* will be used in a context such as "even if I go
now"— *hatta law roht daheen*.

House – Bait
In / at - Fee
Car – Sayara
Already – Aslan
Good morning – Sabah alkhair
How are you? – (M) Kaif halak? (f) kaif halek?
Where are you from? – (M) Men fain enta? (F) men fain enty?
Today – Alyoum
Hello - Hala
What is your name? – (M) Esh esmak? / **(F)** esh esmek?
How old are you? - (M) Kam 'omrak? / (F) kam 'omrek?
Son – Walad
Daughter –Bent
To have – (M) 'Endo/ (F) 'endaha
Doesn't - Ma
Hard – Sa'ab
Still – Lesaa'
With – Maa'
Then (or *"so"*) – Yan'e / fa

She doesn't have a car, so maybe she is still at the house?
Heye ma 'enda seyara, fa balken heye lesaa' fel bait?
I am in the car already with your son and daughter
Ana fel sayara aslan maa' ebnak wa bentak
Good morning, how are you today?
Sabah alkhair, kaif halak al youm?
Hello, what is your name?
Hala, esh esmak (M); Esmek (F)?
How old are you?
Kam 'omrak?
This is very hard, but it's not impossible
Da marra sa'b bas mo mostaheel
Then where are you from?
Ya'ny min fain enta (M); Enty (F)?

*In Arabic, possessive pronouns become suffixes to the noun. For example, in the translation for "your," *bak* is the masculine form, and *bek* is the feminine form.
   * "your book" / (m.) *ktabak.*, (f.) *ktabek*
   * "your house" / *beetak* (m.), *beetek* (f.)

*In the Arabic language, as well as in other Semitic languages, the article "a" doesn't exist. "She doesn't have **a** car" / *heye* (she) *ma* (doesn't) *'endaa* (have) *sayara* (car).

Thank you – Shokran

For – 'Ashan

Anything – Ay haja

That / That is – Hada / hade / daak

Time – Wagt

But – Bas

No / not – La / mo

I am not – Ana mo

Away - B'eed

Late - T'akher

Similar – Nafs / (M) yeshbah *(or)* (F) teshbah

Another/ other – Gheer, a tanye

Side – Janeb / jeha

Until – Lhad

Yesterday – Ams

Without us – Min gherna

Since - Men

Day - Youm

Before – Gabl

Thanks for everything
Shokran'ala kol haja

It's almost time
Tagreeban al wagt

I am not here, I am away
Ana mo hena daheen, ana b'eed

That is a similar house
Hada nafs albaitmgnhfx

I am from the other side
Ana min el jeha attanyia

But I was here until late yesterday Bas ana kont hena lhad a'akhrat ams **I am not at the other house**
Ana mo fel bait a thany

*In Hijazi Arabic, there are three definitions for time:
  * "time" / *waget* refers to "moment period," "duration of time."
  * "time(s)" / *mara / marret)* refers to "occasion" or "frequency."
  * "time" / *kaam el sa'a* references "hour," "what time is it?"

*In Saudi Arabic, there are two separate cases used to signify "side": *janeb* and *jeha*. For "I am from the other side" *jeha*, but for "I stand by your side" here "your side" is *janbak*.

*In Saudi Hijazi Arabic, there are three forms to signify the case of "no"; *la*, *ma*, and *mo*.

La is simply "no"; such as when you say "Can we go outside? No." *Momkn netla' bara?La.*

Ma is "I won't. I won't do this." *Ana ma ha'mel haadak.*

Mo is "I am not / she is not / he is not / they are not" etc. "I am not going" – *ana mo rayeh* / "they are not going" –*homma mo rayheen.*

*To represent "similar" you can either use *yeshbah* or *nafs*, depending on the context: "Similar place" – *nafs al makan;* "they look the same" – *yeshbaho ba'ad.*

This isn't a phrase book! The purpose of this book is solely to provide you with the tools to create your own sentences!

What time is it? – Kaam el sa'a?
I say - Ana bgool
I want – Abgha
Without you – (M) Min gherak / (F) min gherek
Everywhere /wherever – Fi kol makan / ay makan
I go - (M) Brooh / (F) betrooh
With - Maa'
My – Haagy
Cousin - (S)(M) Wald 'aamy, (F) bent 'aamy
I need – Ana mihtaj
Right now – Daheen
Night – Leel
To see - Nshoof
Light - Noor
Outside – Kharej / barra
Without - Bedoon
Happy - Mabsoot
I see / I am seeing - Bshoof

I am saying no / I say no
Bgoool la
I want to see this today
Abgha shoofak alyoum
I am with you everywhere
Ana ma'aak fi kol makan
I am happy without my cousins here
Ana mabsoot bedoon welad 'aamy hena
I need to be there at night
Ana abgha akoon hnaka fillail
I see light outside
Ana shayef annor barra
What time is it right now?
Gadeesh el saa'a daheen?

*"My" / *Haagy* is also a possessive pronoun. *Haagy* means "my" but also becomes a suffix to a noun. Nouns ending with a consonant end with *eh*, for example:
*   "cousin" / *Iben el 'amm*, "my cousin" / *Iben 'ammah*
*   "cup" / *koub*, "my cup" / *kouby*

For second and third person masculine noun, *ibin* ("son"), male (S) *ak, (P) kom*) and female (S) *ik, (P) kum*). "His" – *Ilo* / "hers" – *ila*, noun endings will be *o* (for male) and *a* (for female).

*   "your son" / *ibnak* (m.), *ibnik* (f.)
*   "your (plural) son" / *ibnakum* (m.), *bintakum* (f.)
*   "his son" / *ibno*, "her son" / *ibnaha*
*   "our son" / *ibenna*
*   "their son" / *ibnahom* (m.), *bentahom* (f.)

For second and third person feminine noun: "car" / *seyyara*.

*   "your car" / *sayyaratak*
*   "your (plural) car" / *sayyaratkom*
*   "his car" / *sayyarato*
*   "her car" / *seyyareta sayyarat ha*
*   "our car" / *seyyaretna sayyaratna*
*   "their car" / *sayyarathom* (m.), *sayyarathom* (f.)

53

Place – Makaan
Easy – Sahel
To find - Tlaagy
To look for / to search – Shoof
Near / Close - Greeb
To wait - Entather
To sell - Abee'
To use - Eshtakhdem
To know - E'ref
To decide – Agarer
Between – Mabeen
Both – Al-etnain
To – La
Next to – Janb

This place it's easy to find
Haad el makaan sahel tlaagy
I want to look for this next to the car
Ana abgha ashoof haada elly janeb el seyara
I am saying to wait until tomorrow
Ana bgool nestana elain bokra
This table is easy to sell
Hade el tawle sahel tenbaa'
I want to use this
Ana abgha estakhdem haade
I need to know where is the house
Ana ebgha a'aref fain el bait
I want to decide between both places
Ana ebgha agarer been el makaneen
Where is the bus station?
Fain mahattet el baas?

Because – 'Ashan
To buy – Eshtree
They – Humma
Them, their – Ashanahum
Bottle – Gzaza
Beach – Bahar
Book - Ktab
Mine - Hagety
To understand - Efham
Problem - Moshkela
I do / I am doing - Saweet / bsawee
Of - Men
To look – Shayef / yeshbah
Myself - Nafsy
Enough – Kfaya / khalas *(as in "stop")*
Food / water – Akel / moya
Each/ every/ entire/ all – Kol
Hotel - Fondog

I like this hotel because I want to look at the beach
Ana ahob haad el fondoog 'ashan abgha ashoof el baher
I want to buy a bottle of water
Abgha eshtree garoorat mooya
I do this every day
Ana bsawey keda kol youm
Both of them have enough food
Eletnen 'andhom akl kfaya
That is the book, and that book is mine
Haad howe el ketab, wa haad el keetab haagy
I need to understand the problem
Ana abgha afham el moshkelah
I see the view of the city from the hotel
Ana shayef manzar el madinah min el fondoog
I do my homework today
Ana asawe el wajebaat el youm
My entire life (*all my life***)**
Kol hayaty

*"Both of them" is *letnen*

*There are two ways of saying "life" in Arabic: *"omor* and *hayaah*

55

I like – Ahob / ye'jebny
There is / there are – Fee
Family / Parents – Elahel
Why – Laish
To say – Gool
Something – Haja
To go – Rooh / atla' (as in to "go outside")
Ready – Jahez
Soon – Besora'a
To work – E'mel
Who – Meen
To know - 'Aaref
That (conjunction) – Inno, eza
Important – Mohem

I like to be at my house with my parents
Ana ahob akoon fel bait ma' ahly
I want to know why I need to say something important
Ana abgha a'reef leesh lazm agool shai mohem
I am there with him
Ana kont ma'aah
I am busy, but I need to be ready soon
Ana mashgool bas abgha akoon jahez besora'a
I like to go to work
Ana ye'jebny arooh lel 'amal
'Who is there?
Meen henak?
I want to know if they are here, because I want to go outside
Ana abgha a'ref law hom hena ashan abgha etlaa'atlaa' barra
There are seven dolls
Fee sab' 'arayes
I need to know that that is a good idea
Ana abgha a'ref inno haade fekra helwa

*In the last sentence, we use "that" as a conjunction (*inno*) and a demonstrative pronoun *(M) hada/ (F) hade*.
However, in Saudi dialect, when "that" is used as a conjunction, it can either be *inno* or *eza*. "That that" is *inno* and "that" alone is *eza*.
"I need to know that that is a good idea." *Ana ebgha e'ref inno haade fekra helwa.* "However, I need to know that he is at home." *Ana ebgha e'ref eza howe fel beet.*

How much /how many – Gaadesh *(or)* kam see'ro
To bring – Jeeb
With me - Ma'aya
Instead - Badal
Only – Bas da
When – Lamma /mata
Or – Aw
I can / Can I – Agdar
Were - Kaano
Without me – Men gairy
Fast - Gawaam
Slow – Shwayia shwayia
Cold – Bared
Inside – Jowa
To eat – Akul
Hot – Haar
To Drive – Soog

How much money do I need to bring with me?
Gaadesh feloos mehtaaj ajeeb m'aya?
Instead of this cake, I want that cake
Badal hadeek el keka, ebgha haade el keka
Only when you can
Bas da lama tegdar
They were without me yesterday
Kaano min gheery ams
Do I need to drive the car fast or slow?
Tebgha asoog el sayara bsor'a walla shwaya shwaya?
It is cold inside the library
Eljaw bared fel maktaba
Yes, I like to eat this hot for my lunch
Ewa ana ahob akol el ghada haar
I can work today
Ana agdaar ashtagil el youm

*"Were" is *kanno*, but for "they were," *kano*, "we were" is *konna*.

*"I can" and "can I?" could either be *ana agdar*. "You can" or "can you?" is *tegdar?*

To answer - Jawab
To fly - Teer
Time / Times – Maraa / marrat
To travel – Saafer
To learn - Et'alaam
How – Kaif
To swim - Tesbah
To practice - Mares
To play – El'aab
To leave - Yetrok
Many /much /a lot – Kateer
I go to – Barooh
First – Alawal
I must – Lazem

I want to answer many questions
Ana ebgha ajaweb 'ala as'ela kateer
I must fly to Dubai today
Ana laazem asafer le dubai elyoum
I need to learn how to swim at the pool
Ana ebgha et'alam elsebaha fi al masbah
I want to learn to play better tennis
Ana ebgha et'alam tennis ahsan
I want to leave this here for you when I travel the world
Ana abgha aseeb dee luk lama asafer el'alam
Since the first time
Men awal mara
The children are yours
Alawlad hoggonak

*In Hijazi Arabic, "to leave (something)" is *yetrok*. "To leave (a place)" is *yetrok* or *yemshy* or *seeb*.

*In Hijazi Arabic, there are three definitions for time:
   * "time" / *wagt* refers to "era", "moment period," "duration of time."
   * "time(s)" / *marra(t)* refers to "occasion" or "frequency."
   * "time" / *sa'a* references "hour," "what time is it?"

Hagak (f.) *hagek*, literally means "your", "yours", or used in cases to represent something which belongs to "you."

With the knowledge you've gained so far, now try to create your own sentences!

Nobody / anyone – Ma fee ahad / had
Against - Ded
Us – Ehna
To visit - Zeyara / yezoor
Mom – Omm
To give – A'aty
Which – Ay
To meet - Tgabel / tejtame
Someone – Hadaak / hada
Just - Bas
Walk - Barma / nemshy
Around – Hawalen
Than - Men
Nothing – Mafe sheey / wala shey

Something is better than nothing
Shaay ahsan min wala shey
I am against him
Ana dedo
Is there anyone here?
Fee had hena?
We go to visit my family each week
Ehna bnrooh nezoor el ahl kol osboo'aa
I need to give you something
Ana abgha a'ateek haja
Do you want to go meet someone?
Tebgha trooh tgabel hadaak?
I was here on Wednesdays as well
Ana kont hena youm el roboo'
Do you do this everyday?
Enta betsawe keda kol youm?
You need to walk towards the house
Enta lazem tsawe barma betejah al bait

*In Arabic, when using the pronoun "you" as a direct and indirect object pronoun (the person who is actually affected by the action that is being carried out) in relation to a verb, the pronoun "you" becomes a suffix to that verb. That suffix becomes *ak* (masc.) *ik* (fem.).

* "to give" / *te'teh* : "to give you" / *ta a'teek*
* "to tell" / *gool*: "to tell you" / *goolak* (m.), goolek(f.)
* "see you" / *shoofak*: "to see you" (plural) / *shoofkom shofakom* (m.), *shoofkon* (f.)

For third person male, add *o* and *om* for plural, for female add *ha* and *om* for plural.

* "tell him" / *gollo*
* "tell her" / *gollaha*
* "see them" / *shofahom* (m.), *shofahom* (f.)
* "see us " / *shoofana*

I have – 'Endy
Don't - La / ma
Friend – As-haby
To borrow – Astalef
To look like / resemble – Yeshbah
Like (preposition) – Nafs
Grandfather – Jaddi (Father side), Sidi (Mother Side)
To want – Abgha
To stay - Estana
To continue – Akamel
I don't – Ana ma / ana mo
Way – Tareeg
To show - Twary / tfarej
To prepare - Et-hadar
I am not going – Ana many rayeh
Incorrect – Mo tamaam / mo mazboot

Do you want to look like Salim
Tebgha Tseer teshbeh saleem?
I want to borrow this book for my grandfather
Ana abgha astalef haad el ketab ashan jeddy
I want to drive and to continue on this way to my house
Ana abgha asoog wa akamel 'ala thak el tareeg ela baity
I have a friend there, that's why I want to stay in the Gulf
Ana sahebi hnak, 'ashan keda abgha ag'ood fe al-khaleej
I am not going to see anyone here
Ana ma abgha ashoof ahad hena
I need to show you how to prepare breakfast
Ana abgha awarreek kaif tsawy el fotoor
Why don't you have the book?
Leesh mo indak el ketab?
That is incorrect, I don't need the car today
La mo tamam, ana mo mihtaaj el seyara elyoum

Ala thaak is "on this."

60

To remember – Tethakar Tet-thakar
Your - (F) Ek / (M) ak / (M) hagaak (F) hagek
Number – Ragam
Hour – Saa'a
Dark / darkness – Thalaam
Arabic – Araby
About – Fe / 'an
Grandmother – Jaddati (Father side), Sitti (Mother side)
Five - Khamsa
Minute / minutes – Dgeega / dgayeg
More - Ktheer/ akthar
To think – Faker
To do – A'mol / asawe
To come – Yejy
To hear - Esma'
Last – Elakheer

You need to remember my number
Enta mihtaj tethakar ragmy
This is the last hour of darkness
Haady akher sa'a min elthalam
**I want to come and to hear my grandmother speak
Arabic** Ana abgha 'aji wa asma' sitti Tetkallam 'araby
I need to think more about this, and what to do
Ana abgha afaker akthar fe hada, wa esh asawy
From here to there, it's only five minutes
Min hena lehnak, bas khams dgayeg
The school on the mountain
Almadrasa 'ala el jabal

*In Saudi Arabic *B-khsoos* / is used to signify about, for example "let's talk about this topic," *nehky fel mawdoo' hada*. However, on the mountain" is a place, so in this case we will use *'ala*.
*This *isn't* a phrase book! The purpose of this book is *solely* to provide you with the tools to create *your own* sentences!

To leave - Etrok
Again – Mara thanya
Saudi Arabia - El mamlaka el 'arabya el s'odya (Literal meaning is "the Saudi Arabian Kingdom")
Jeddah – Jedda
Wake up – Es-ha
To take - Akhod
To try - Jareb
To rent – Asta'jer
Without her – Men gherha
We are – Ehna
To turn off - Sakker
To ask – Es'al
To stop - Wagef
Permission - Esta'then
To sleep - Naam
To pray - Salee

He needs to leave and rent a house at the beach
Howa mihtaj yetrok wa yesta'jer bait ala ashati
I want to take the test without her
Ana abgha akhod el ekhtebar men gheraha
We are here a long time
Ehna hena min zamaan
I need to turn off the lights early tonight
Ana abgha atafy al anwar badree el leela
We want to stop here
Ehna nebgha nwagef hena
We are from Jeddah
Ehna min Jedda
The same building
Nafs el mabna
I want to ask permission to leave
Ana abgha akhod ethen wa etrok
I want to go on the Hajj in Saudi Arabia
Ana abgha arooh 'ala al hajj fel mamlaka el 'arabya el s'odya
I need to go to sleep now so I can wake up early because I need to pray at the Masjid al-Haram mosque
Ana mihtaj arooh anam daheen ashan agdar as-ha bokrah abgha asalee fi al masjed al haraam
I need to walk around the Kaaba seven times
Ana mihtaj atoof hawaleen al kaaba al musharrafah saba'a marra

To open - Eftah
A bit, a little, a little bit - Shwaya
To pay – Edfaa'
Once again – Mara thanya
There isn't/ there aren't – Ma fee / ma fee shay
Sister – Okht
To hope - Etmana
To live – A'eesh / saken
Nice to meet you – Tsharafna b ma'reftak
Name – Esm
Last name – Esm el 'a'ila
To return – Yerjaa' / yrajaa'
Door – Baab

I need to open the door for my sister
Ana abgha eftah el baal le okhty
I need to buy something
Ana abgha eshtery haja
I want to meet your sisters
Ana abgha agabil akhwatak
Nice to meet you, what is your name and your last name?
Tsharaft b ma'reftak, esh esmak wa esm 'ayltak?
To hope for a little better
Etmana haja ahsan
I want to return from the United States and to live in Qatar without problems
Ana abgha arjaa' min america wa 'aish fee gatar bedoon mashakel
Why are you sad right now?
Leesh enta za'lan daheen?
There aren't any people here
Ma fee ay naas hena
There isn't enough time to go to Mecca and Medina today
Mafee wagt kaafy nrooh le makka wa al-maddina elyoum

*"To return" – *Yerjaa'* / *yrajaa'* (The usage depends on the context. If it's regarding the return from a place, *yerjaa'* will be used. If it's to return something, then it's *yrajaa'*.)

*In Hijazi Arabic, "to live (as to exist)" is *a'eesh*. "To live (as in to live in a place)" is *saken*.

*In Hijazi Arabic, regarding the verb "to meet" there are two separate cases to define this verb; *tgabil* and *tejteme'*. Depending of the context: to meet for business is *tejteme'* like in the sentence "do you want to go meet someone?" However, for meeting the sister, is getting acquainted with her, here it's *gabil*.

To happen – Yehsal /yeseer
To order – Etlob
Excuse me – Law samaht
Child – Tefel (Bazor)
Woman - Horma
To begin / to start - Yebdaa'
To finish – Yekhalles
To help - Yesa'ed
To smoke – Yedakhen
To love – Hob
To talk / to speak – Yetkallam

This must happen today
Lazem hatha yeseer el youm
Excuse me, my child is here as well
Law samaht, Waladi (son), Binty (daughter) hena kaman
I love you
Ana ahobak
I see you
Ana shayfak
I need you at my side
Ana abghak jamby
I need to begin soon to be able to finish at 3 o'clock in the afternoon Ana abgha abda badree 'ashan akhales ala assa'ah 3 ba'd el thohr
I need help
Ana abghak tsa'edny
I don't want to smoke once again
Ana ma abgha adakhen mara thanya
I want to learn how to speak Arabic
Ana abgha ata'llam kaif atkallam 'araby
I need to take a taxi to the airport
Ana mihtej aakhod taxi lil matar

*"To help" is *sa'ed*. However, "help!" is *mosa'ada*. "I need help" or "I need rescue" / *ana meh'teij mosa'ada*.

*"To be able to" is *'ashan*.

To read – Yegra
To write – Yektub
To teach - Ye'alem
To close – Yesakker
To choose – Yektar
To prefer – Yefaddel
To put – Yhot
Less - Agal
Sun - Shams
Month – Shahr
I talk - Btkalam
Exact – Sah / nafs

I need this book to learn how to read and write in Arabic because I want to teach in Kuwait
Ana abgha hada al ketab 'ashan atallam kaif egra agra wa aktub bel 'araby 'ashan abgha adarres fe l-Kwait
I want to close the door of the house
Ana abgha asakker baab el bait
I prefer to put the gift here
Ana afadel ahot el hena
I want to pay less than you for the dinner
Ana ebgha abgha edfaa' adfaa' agal menak fel 'asha
There is sun outside today
Fee shams barra el youm

*"In" is bel.

*"For the" is *fel.*

*"Exact" – *Sah / nafs* (The usage depends on the context. If it's pertaining to the exact place then it's *nafs*, but if it's exactly then it's *sah*.)

*With the knowledge you've gained so far, now try to create your own sentences!

To exchange (money) – Sarf / Yesref
Brother – Akh
Dad – Ab
To sit – Yeg'ood
Together – Ma' ba'd
To change – Taghyeer
Of course - Akeed
Welcome - Hala
During - Khelal
Years - Sneen
Sky - Sama
Up – Foog
Down - Taht
Sorry – Ma'lesh
Big – Kabeer
New – Jadeed
Never / ever - Abadan
To call – Yesa'l / Yetasel
To the – Lel, ila
To follow - Ilhag
During – Wast

I don't want to exchange this money at the bank
Ana ma abgha asref el feloos fel bank
Of course I can come to the theater, and I want to sit together with you and with your sister
Akeed agdar 'ajy el masrah, wa abgha ag'od ma'ak enta wa okhtak
I need to go down to see your new house
Ana abgha anzel taht wa ashoof beetak el jdeed
I can see the sky from the window
Ana agder shoof el sama min el shobbak
I am sorry, but he wants to follow her to the store
Ma'lesh, howa yebgha yemshy waraha lel mahal
I don't ever want to see you again
Ma abgha ashofak mara thanya

*In Saudi dialect, brother is *akh,* and dad is *ab*. However, "my dad" is *aboya* and "my brother" is *khooy akhooya*. "My sister" is *okhty*, and "my mother" is *ommy*

*In Saudi Arabic, "to call (out to someone)" is *yes'al*. "To call (on the phone)" is *etasel*.

To allow – Yesmah
To believe – Sadeg
Morning – Nahar *(or)* sabah
Except - Ma 'ada
To promise - Yo'ed
Good night - Tesbah 'ala kheir
To recognize - Ye'ref
People - Naas / khalg
To move - Engol
Far - B'eed
Different – Gheir / mokhtalef
Man – Rejjal
To enter - Yedkhol
To receive – Yestalem
Throughout - Khelal
Good evening – Ma-sa' el kheir
Left / right - Yasaar / yemeen
Him / her - O / a (read footnote)

I need to allow him to go with us, he is a different man now
Ane mihtaj asmahlo yrooh ma'ana, la'enno howa rijjal mokhtalef al'an
I believe everything except this
Ana msaddeg kol haja ma 'ada hada
I promise to say good night to my parents each night
Ana Awed enni agool tisbaho 'ala kheir le ahly koll leyleh
The people from Jordan are very pleasant
A nass illi men el ordon kteer tayebeen
I need to find another hotel very quickly
Ana mihtaj alagi fondog tany bsor'a
They need to receive a book for work
Homa mihtajeen yestalmo ketab le ashogol
I see the sun in the morning
Ana bashoof ashshams fi nahar
The house is on the right side of the street
El bait 'ala yemeen el share'

*For the possessive pronouns, her (*a*) and him (*o*), both become suffixes to the verb or noun. Concerning nouns: "her house" / *bet-ha*, "his house" / *beito*. However, concerning cases regarding verbs, please see page 19.

To wish - Etmana
Bad - Mo Tayeb
To get – Akhod / tjeeb
To forget - Insa
Everybody / Everyone - Kol shakhs / Kollahum
Although - Ma' inno
To feel - Hess
Great – Mohem
Next (as in close, near) - Janb / gareeb
Next (as in next year) - Jai
To like – Ye'jeb
In front – Gedam
Person - Shakhes
Behind - Wara
Well - Ahsan
Restaurant - Mat'aam
Bathroom - Hamaam / doret moya
Goodbye - Ma' elsalama

I don't want to wish you anything bad
Ana ma abgha atmanna lak ay shi mo tayeb
I must forget everybody from my past to feel well
Ana lazem insa kol shakhs min almady 'ashan ahess zein bekhair
I am next to the person behind you
Ana janb el elshaks elly warak
There is a great person in front of me
Fi shaks 'atheem geddamy
I say goodbye to my friends
Ana bgooul ma' el salama le (as-haby)
Where is the bathroom in the restaurant?
Fain Alhammam fel mat'am?
She has to get a car before the next year
Heya lazem tejeeb sayyarah gabl assanah aljayah
I like the house, but it is very small
Ana Ajebni al bait, bass howa marrah sagheer

Janb literally means "side." In Arabic, it refers to "next." *jannby* is "besides me" and *janbak* is "besides you."

*"To get" as in "take" is *akhod* but "to get" as "to bring" is *tjeeb*.

68

To remove / to take out – Yesheel
Please - Men fedlak / raja'an
Beautiful - (**M**)Helwo, (**F**)helwa
To lift – Erfa' / sheel
Include / Including - Ma'
Belong – Byedkhol / men
To hold - Emsok
To check – It'akkad
Small - Sgheer
Real - Hageegy
Week - Osboo'
Size - Hajm
Even though - Hatta law
Doesn't - Mo
So (as in "then") – Ya'ny
So (as in "so big") - Kteer
Price - Se'er

She wants to remove this door please
Hiyyeh tebgha tsheel haad el baab rajaa'an
This doesn't belong here, I need to check again
Hada mo men hena, ana mijhtaj it'akkad marra tanya
This week the weather was very beautiful
Hadi al Jum'aa Al jao kan marrah helo
We need to check the size of the house
Ehna mihtajeen nit'akkad min hajmel bait
I want to lift this, so you need to hold it high
Ana ebgha Arfa' hada, ya'ny Lazim timseko lefoog
I can pay this even though that the price is expensive
Ana egder idfa' hada hatta la wa inno el se'er ghaly
Including everything is this price correct?
Maa' kol haja, hada ese'er mathboot?

Countries of the Middle East
Bulud Asharg alawsat

Lebanon – Lobnan Lebnan
Syria – Suriyya Suria
Jordan - L-ordon
Saudi Arabia - El mamlaka el 'arabya el s'odya
Israel /Palestine /West Bank - Isra'eel / falasten / al daffa el gharbya
Bahrain - L-Bahrein
Yemen - L-Yaman
Oman - 'Oman
United Arab Emirates - L-Emarat
Kuwait - L-Kweit
Iraq - L-'Irag
Qatar - Gatar
Morocco - Maghreb
Algeria - L-Jazeh'ir
Libya - Leebya
Egypt - Massr
Tunisia - Tunis

Months
January - Ynayr
February - Fbrayr
March – Mares
April - Ebreel
May - Mayo
June - Yonyo
July - Yolyo
August – Ogostos
September - Sebtamber
October - Octobar
November – Novambar
December – Decambar

Days of the Week
Sunday - Ahad
Monday - Ethnein
Tuesday - Tholathaa' (Thalooth)
Wednesday - Roboo' (Arbia'a)
Thursday - Khamees
Friday - Jem'aa
Saturday – Sabt

Seasons
Spring – Rabee'
Summer - Saif
Autumn - Khareef
Winter – Sheta

Cardinal Directions
North - Shamal
South - Janoob
East – Sharg
West – Gharb

Colors

Black - (M) Aswad **(F)** Soda
White - (M) Abyadd **(F)** Byda
Gray - (M) Ramadi **(F)** Ramadiyah
Red - (M) Ahmar **(F)**Hamra
Blue - (M) Azrag **(F)**Zarga
Yellow - (M) Asfar **(F)**Safra
Green - (M) Akhdar **(F)**Khadra
Orange – Bortokani
Purple – Laylaki
Brown - (M) Bonny **(F)** Bonnyiah

Numbers

One – Wahid
Two – Etnain
Three – Talatah
Four - Arb'aa
Five – Khamsah
Six – Sittah
Seven - Sab'aa
Eight - Tmehneh
Nine - Tis'aa
Ten - 'Ashra
Twenty - 'Eshreen
Thirty - Talateen
Hundred – Miyyah
Thousand – Alf
Million - Malyoon

Conversational
Arabic Quick
and easy

SAUDI GULF DIALECT

YATIR NITZANY

THE SAUDI GULF DIALECT

The population of Saudi Arabia is estimated at 33 million people. As with other Arabic countries, Modern Standard Arabic is the standard national language spoken by all. It is a formal language mainly used for government communications and media.

The main languages spoken in the country are Gulf Arabic, the Najdi dialect, and Hijazi.

Although spoken over much of Saudi Arabia's area, Gulf Arabic is not the native tongue of most Saudis. There are some 500,000 Gulf Arabic speakers in the country and they reside mostly in the Eastern Province. There are approximately 8.8 million Gulf Arabic speakers worldwide.

The most populous province, and the largest by area, is the Eastern Province, which is also home to most of Saudi Arabia's oil production and to a global hub for chemical industries. Because of its link with the oil-producing region in Saudi Arabia and the English-speaking oil-production companies and history of the area, there are many English loan words in the language.

Its location on the coast of the Persian Gulf also makes the Eastern Province a tourist area as well. Its capital is the city of Dammam, where most of the region's population live and where the seat of government is hosted. The Eastern Province is the third most populous province in the country, after Makkah and Riyadh. Dammam is the sixth most populous city in the whole of Saudi Arabia.

The remaining Arabic speakers in the province speak one of the other two dialects, more commonly the Najdi dialect.

While Gulf Arabic is mainly spoken by people living in Kuwait, Qatar, and the United Arab Emirates, it is also spoken by a minority of the population of Saudi Arabia and Bahrain, as well as a small pocket of the population of Iraq. Approximately one-third of the population of Oman speaks the Gulf Arabic dialect.

ARABIC PRONUNCIATIONS

PLEASE MASTER THE FOLLOWING PAGE IN ARABIC PRONUNCIATIONS PRIOR TO STARTING THE PROGRAM

Kha. For Middle Eastern languages including Arabic, Hebrew, Farsi, Pashto, Urdu, Hindi, etc., and also German, to properly pronounce the kh or ch is essential, for example, *Khaled* (a Muslim name) or *Chanukah* (a Jewish holiday) or *Nacht* ("night" in German). The best way to describe kh or ch is to say "ka" or "ha" while at the same time putting your tongue at the back of your throat and blowing air. It's pronounced similarly to the sound that you make when clearing your throat. Please remember this whenever you come across any word containing a kh in this program.

Ghayin. The Arabic gh is equivalent to the "g" in English, but its pronunciation more closely resembles the French "r," rather than "g." Pronounce it at the back of your throat. The sound is equivalent to what you would make when gargling water. Gha is pronounced more as "rha," rather than as "ga." *Ghada* is pronounced as "rhada." In this program, the symbol for *ghayin* is gh, so keep your eyes peeled.

Aayin is pronounced as a'a, pronounced deep at the back of your throat. Rather similar to the sound one would make when gagging. In the program, the symbol for *aayin* is *a'a, u'u, o'o,* or *i'i.*

Ha is pronounced as "ha." Pronunciation takes place deep at the back of your throat, and for correct pronunciation, one must constrict the back of the throat and exhale air while simultaneously saying "ha." In the program, this strong h ("ha") is emphasized whenever *ha, ah, hi, he,* or *hu* is encountered.

NOTE TO THE READER

The purpose of this book is merely to enable you to communicate in the Saudi Gulf Arabic dialect. In the program itself (pages 17-38) you may notice that the composition of some of those sentences might sound rather clumsy. This is intentional. These sentences were formulated in a specific way to serve two purposes: to facilitate the easy memorization of the vocabulary and to teach you how to combine the words in order to form your own sentences for quick and easy communication, rather than making complete literal sense in the English language. So keep in mind that this is not a phrase book!

As the title suggests, the sole purpose of this program is for conversational use only. It is based on the mirror translation technique. These sentences, as well as the translations are not incorrect, just a little clumsy. Latin languages, Semitic languages, and Anglo-Germanic languages, as well as a few others, are compatible with the mirror translation technique.

Many users say that this method surpasses any other known language learning technique that is currently out there on the market. Just stick with the program and you will achieve wonders!

Again, I wish to stress this program is by no means, shape, or form a phrase book! The sole purpose of this book is to give you a fundamental platform to enable you to connect certain words to become conversational. Please also read the "Introduction" and the "About Me" section prior to commencing the program.

In order to succeed with my method, please start on the very first page of the program and fully master one page at a time prior to proceeding to the next. Otherwise, you will overwhelm yourself and fail. Please do not skip pages, nor start from the middle of the book.

It is a myth that certain people are born with the talent to learn a language, and this book disproves that myth. With this method, anyone can learn a foreign language as long as he or she follows these explicit directions:

* Memorize the vocabulary on each page

* Follow that memorization by using a notecard to cover the words you have just memorized and test yourself.

* Then read the sentences following that are created from the vocabulary bank that you just mastered.

* Once fully memorized, give yourself the green light to proceed to the next page.

Again, if you proceed to the following page without mastering the previous, you are guaranteed to gain nothing from this book. If you follow the prescribed steps, you will realize just how effective and simplistic this method is.

The Program

Let's Begin! "Vocabulary" (Memorize the Vocabulary)

I | I am - Ana
With you – (M) ana ma'ak/ (F) ana ma'ach
With him / with her - Ma'aah / Ma'aha
With us - Ma'ana
For you - (**Masc**) 'Ashanak / (**Fem**) Ashanech
Without him - Bedonah
Without them - Bedonhom
Always –Dayman
Was – Kan
This, this is, it's, it is – (**M**) Hatha, Hatha ho (**F**) Hathy, Hathy hey **Sometimes** –Ahyanan
Maybe – Yemkin
You / you are / are you – (M) Ent (F) Enty
You (plural) - Entoum
Is it - (M) Wesh ho, (F) Wesh hey
Today – Alyom
Better – Ahsan
He / he is - Ho
She / she is - He
From - Min

This is for you
(M) Hatha ashank (F) Hatha ashanech
I am from Saudi
Ana min al saudia
Are you from Riyadh?
Int min el-Riyadh?
I am with you
(M) Ana ma'ak (F) Ana ma'ach
Sometimes you are with us at the mall
(M) Ahyanan int ma'ana fel mall (F) Ahyanan enty ma'ana fel mall
I am always with her
Ana dayman ma'aha
Are you without them today?
Ent bdonhom alyoum?
Sometimes I am with him
Ahyanan ana ma'ah

*In Saudi Gulf Arabic, with the question "is it?", the "it" can pertain to either a masculine or feminine noun. However, whenever pertaining to a masculine or feminine noun, it will become *ho* or *he*. For example, when referring to a feminine noun such as *sayaara* ("the car), "is it (the car in question) here?" / *he hena?* When referring to a masculine noun such as *kalb* ("a dog), "is it (the dog in question) on the table?" *ho 'ala tawla?* However, I yet again wish to stress that this isn't a grammar book!

I was - Ana kent
To be - (**M**) Ykun / (**F**) Tikun
The - Al
Same – Nafs alhal
Good - Zain
Here - Hena
Very – Hail / Marra
And - W
Between - Bain
Now – Alheen
Later / After / afterwards - Ba'ad / Ba'den
If - Etha
Yes - Iyeh
To – N/ la
Tomorrow – Bokra / Bacher
You - (M) Ent / (F) Enti
Also / too / as well – Ba'ad
With them – Ma'ahom

If it's between now and later
Etha kan bain alheen w ba'deen
It's better tomorrow
Bokra ahsan
This is good as well
Hatha zain ba'ad
To be the same person
Yekon nafs alshakhs
Yes, you are very good
Eh, ent hail zain
I was here with them
Ana knt hena ma'ahom
You and I
Ent w ana
The same day
Nafs alyom

Me - Le
Ok – Tamam / Kuayis
Even if - Hatta law / Hatha etha
No – lla
Worse – Aswa'
Where - Wain
Everything – Kel shi
Somewhere – Ay mkan
What –Aish? / Shno?
Almost - Tagriban
There - Henak

Afterwards is worse
Ba'aden aswa'
Even if I go now
Hatta law arooh alheen
Where is everything?
Wain kelshai?
Maybe somewhere
Yimken fi makan
What? I am almost there
Aish? Ana taqreban henak
Where are you?
(M) Wheynak? (F) Wheynach?
Where is the airport?
Wain el matar?

*"There" has two meanings, *fe* or *hnak* depending on the context, when we say there is we say *fe* / but when we say "I am there (place)" we say *ana hnak*.

* *makan* literally means *in a place*

* In Arabic, the pronoun "me" has several definitions. In relation to verbs, it's *le*. *Le* refers to any verb that relates to the action of doing something to someone or for someone.
For example, "tell me," "tell (to) me" / (M) *gool le*.
'ni' just means "me": "love me" / *hebbni*
Other variations (*ya*):
   * "on me" / *'aleya,* "in me" / *fiya*
   * "to me" / *'leya,* "with me" / *ma'aya*

The same rule applies for "him" and "her"—both become suffixes: *–o* and *–a*. Basically all verbs pertinent to males end with *h*, and all pertinent to female end with ha.
   * "love her" / *ahebha*
   * "love him" / *ahebbah*
   * "love them" / *ahebhom*
   * "love us" / *ahebbna*
Any verb that relates to doing someone to someone, for someone put *l*:
   * "tell her" / *gel-lha*
   * "tell him" / *gel-lh*
   * "tell them" / *gel-lhom*
   * "tell us" / *qel-lna*
Adding you as a suffix in Arabic is *ak* or *lak,* female *ik* or *lik*.
   * "love you" / (M) *ahebbak* / (F) *ahebbech*
   * "tell you" / (M) *agol-lk* / (F) *agol-lch*

House - Bait
In / at - Fe / A'la
Car - Seyyara
Already – Aslan
Good morning - Sabah el kheir
How are you? – Shlonak? (F)Shlonach? Shakhbarek? (F) Shakhbarich?
Where are you from? – (M) Min wain ent? (F) Min wain enti?
Today - Alyom
Hello - Ahlan
What is your name? – (M) Shesmek? (F) Shesmich?
How old are you? - (M) Kam omrak? / (F) Kam omrich?
Son – Wald
Daughter - Bnt
To have – (M)'Endah / (F) 'Endha
Doesn't – Ma / La
Hard – Sa'ab
Still – **(M)** Baqi / (F) Baqia lelheen
Then (or "so") – Ba'ad/ W ba'ad
In order to – 'Ashan

She doesn't have a car, so maybe she is still at the house?
Ma endaha seyyara, yemkin lelheen fel bait?
I am in the car already with your son and daughter
Ana bel/fel seyyara aslan ma'a wldak w bntak
Good morning, how are you today?
Sabah al kheir, (M) Shlonak/(F) Slonach alyoum?
Hello, what is your name?
Hala, (M) Shesmek / (F) Shemich?
How old are you?
Kam omrak/ (F) omrich?
This is very hard, but it's not impossible
Hatha sa'ab heel, bas mub mustaheel
Then where are you from?
Min wain ent?

*In Arabic, possessive pronouns become suffixes to the noun. For example, in the translation for "your," *ak* is the masculine form, and *ich* is the feminine form. *Ich/ ach*
   * "your book" / *ktabak* (m.), *ktabik* (f.) *ktabich*
   * "your house" / *baitak* (m.), *baitik* (f.) *baitich*
*In Saudi Arabic *a* is used to indicate cases of "to" or "to be able to." You will notice in the program *ka* will quite often become a prefix to the verb "I want to learn," *ana abe at'alem* or "in order to be able to go". *Ashan agdar arooh*

Ashan means "because of," but it is also used to indicate "so."

Thank you - Mashkur
For – 'Ashan
Anything - Ay Shay / kl shay
That / That is – (F) Hathik / (M) Hathak (F) Theek (M) Thak
Time - Zaman (duration) / Sa'a (if asking about the clock) Wagt (duration)
But - W laken / Bas
No / not - La / Mu
I am not - Ana la / Ma
Away - B'eed
Late – Meta'kher
Similar – Methl / Zay Nafs
Another/ other – Thany / Ghair **Side –** Jnb / Yam
Until – Elen / Lain
Yesterday – Elbareh / Ams
Without us – Bdon-na
Since – Min wagt ma
Day - Youm
Before – Gabl

Thanks for everything
Mashkur ala kl Shay
It's almost time
Hatha alwagt tagreban
I am not here, I am away
Ana mub hena, ana b'eed
That is a similar house
Hatha methl albait
I am from the other side
Ana min makan thany
But I was here until late yesterday Bas ana knt hena len allail ams a'kher **I am not at the other house**
Ana mu fe albait althany

*In Arabic *mojood* literally means "to exist" or "is present."
*In Saudi Arabic regarding negations, such as "no", "not", "doesn't", "can't", "don't" it's either *ma* or *la*. *La* is used to indicate cases such as "are you here" ent hena then you reply "no" *la*. is used to indicate cases of "not," "doesn't," "don't," for example: "I am not at the other house" is *ana mu fi albait el athani*. In some instances both cases of *la* may be used, for example; "can you come?" "No I can't" *la ma haqder*.
*In Saudi Arabic, there are three definitions for time:
  * "time" / *mudda* refers to "era", "moment period," "duration of time."
  * "time(s)" / *marra(t)* / wagt *(t)* refers to "occasion" or "frequency."
*"time" / *sa'a* references "hour," "what time is it?" Time, *sa'ah* in reference to; hour, what time is it.
This isn't a phrase book! The purpose of this book is solely to provide you with the tools to create your own sentences!

What time is it? – Kam al sa'aa?
I say / I am saying – Agool /
Ana agool-lk/ (F) Agool-lch
I want Ana abe / Abe
Without you – **(M)** Bdoonak /
(F) Bedonich
Everywhere /wherever – Kl
makan **I go** – Barooh
With - Ma'a
My – Le
Cousin (paternal) - (M) Wld
'amy / (F) Bnt 'amy / (P)(F)
Banaat 'amy
(P)(M) Awlad 'amy/ 'Aiyal 'amy
Cousin (maternal) - (M) Wld
khaly /(F) Bnt khali / (P)(M)
Wlaad khaly /(P)(F) Banaat khaly
(P)(M) Awlad khaly/'Aiyal khaly
I need – Ahtaj
Right now – Alheen
Night – Lail
To see – 'Ashan ashoof
Light - Noor
Outside – Barra / 'Ala barra
Without – Bala / Bdoon
Happy – Farhan / Saeed Mistanes
I see / I am seeing – Anadher /
Ashoof
I am saying no / I say no -
Agool la'

I want to see this today
Abe ashof hatha alyom
I am with you everywhere
Ana (M) ma'ak (F) ma'ach Fe kl
makan
**I am happy without my cousins
here**
Ana sa'ed bdoon Awlad 'ammy hna
I need to be there at night
Ahtaj akoon hnak be allail
I see light outside
Ashoof noor barra
What time is it right now?
Kam alsa'aa alheen?

*"Mine" /*haggi, maly*/ is also a possessive pronoun. Haggi/Maly *Haggi* means "my" but also becomes a suffix to a noun. Nouns ending in a vowel end with –*the*. Nouns ending with a consonant end with –*eh*. For example:

"cousin" / *iben el 'amm*, "my cousin" / *iben 'ammy*, "cup" / *cob*, "my cup" / *cobi* For second and third person masculine noun, *ibin* ("son"), male (S) *ak*, (P) *kom*) and female (S) *ich* (P) *kum*). "His" – *ilo* / "hers" – *ila*, noun endings will be *o* (for male) and *a* (for female).

"your son" / *ibnak* (m.), *ibnik* (f.), "your (plural) son" / *ibinkom* (m.), *bintkom* (f.), "his son" / *ibnoh*, "her son" / *ibnha*, "our son" / ibnna , "their son" / ibbnhom (m.), ibnnhon(f.)

For second and third person feminine noun: "car" / *seyyara*.

* "your car" / *seyyartek*, "your (plural) car" / *seyyartkom*, "his car" / *seyyartah*, "her car" / *seyyartha*, "our car" / *seyyaratna*, "their car" / *seyyarthom*

Place – Makan
Easy - Sahel
To find - (M) Yelga / (F)Telga
To look for / to search – Yedawwer
Near / Close - Garib
To wait – Yestanna / yentdher
To sell - (M) Ybee' - (F) tbee'
To use – Yesta'amel
To know – Y'arf
To decide – Yqarrir
Between - Bain
Both – Thnain
To – 'Ashan (preceding a verb)

This place it's easy to find
Hatha almkan sahel algah
I want to look for this next to the car
Ana abe adawer janb alseyyara
I am saying to wait until tomorrow
Ana agool nentedher len bokra
This table is easy to sell
Hathi altawla sahel tenba'
I want to use this
Abe asta'mel hathi
I need to know where is the house
Ahtaj a'aref wain albait
I want to decide between both places
Abe aqrrer bain almkanen

* *Lazim* means "must" however in this program, both, *lazim* and *ahtaj* will be used interchangeably.
* In Saudi Gulf Arabic, in the event "doesn't" is used regarding negations of verbs, the following requirements must precede and follow *ma.. mat.. ha,* for example: "she doesn't like (The verb "like" is ye'*jeb*) the beer" – *hey ma te'ajbha lbeera.*

Because – 'Ashan
To buy – Ashtry
They - Hum
Them | Their – Hum / Haghum/Malhum/hum
Bottle – Qarora / Gharsha
Book - Kitab
Mine - Haggi
To understand – Yefham
Problem / Problems - (S) Mushkila / Meshakel
I do / I am doing - N'mel / A'amel Asawy
Of - Mn
To look – Yshoof
Myself - Nafsi
Enough – Khalas / Kafi
Food / water - Akil / Moya
Each/ every/ entire/ all – Kl
Hotel - Fondoq

I like this hotel because I want to look at the beach
Ajbni hatha alfondoq ashan weddi ashoof alshate'a
I want to buy a bottle of water
Ana abe ashtry gharshat maay
I do this everyday
Ana asawy chetha kl youm
Both of them have enough food
Ethnenhom endhom akl kafi
That is the book, and that book is mine
Hatha alktab, w hatha alktab haggi
I need to understand the problem
Ana ahtaj afham almushkila
I see the view of the city from the hotel
Ashoof mandhar almadina mn alfondoq
I do my homework today
Asawy wajbati alyoum
My entire life (*all my life*)
Kl hayati / kl omri

I like – Ye'jbni
There is / There are – Fe
Family / Parents - 'Aylah / Walidin / Ahel
Why – Laish
To say – Agool / (M) Ygool / (F) Tgool
Something – Haja / Shai
To go – Nmshy / (M) Yimshy / (F) Timshy
Ready – Jahiz
Soon – Gareeb
To work – Ashteghil / (M) Yeshteghil / (F) Teshteghil
Who – Meen
To know – A'aref
That (conjunction) – Ennah

I like to be at my house with my parents
Aheb akon bilbait ma' ahle
I want to know why I need to say something important
Ana weddi a'aref laish ana ahtaj agool shai mohem
I am there with him
Ana hnak ma'ah
I am busy, but I need to be ready soon
Ana mashghool, bass ahtaj akon jahiz gareb
I like to go to work
Ye'ajbni aroh al amal / alshghl
'Who is there?
Meen hnak?
I want to know if they are here, because I want to go outside
Ana abe a'aref etha hom hena, ashan abe arooh barra / weddi atla'a
There are seven dolls
Fee sab'a al'ab
I need to know that it is a good idea
Ahtaj a'aref ennah fekra zaina

*In the last sentence, we use "that" as a conjunction (*ennah*) and a demonstrative pronoun *(M) hatha* / *(F) theek*).

How much /how many – Kam / Gad esh
To bring – Ajeb
With me – Ma'aya
Instead - Badal
Only – Bass / Lamma
When – Mita
Or – Aw
I can / Can I – Ana agdar / Mumken?/ 'Adey? / Agdar?
Were - Kano
Without me - Bdooni
Fast – Bser'aa
Slow – Batee / Shway / B-shwaysh
Cold – Bard
Inside – Jowwa / Dakhel / Fee
To eat – 'Aakil
Hot – Haar
To Drive – Aswog
To drive - Yasouk

How much money do I need to bring with me?
Kam ajeeb ma'ay floos?
Instead of this cake, I want that cake
Badal hathi al caikah, abe hathi al caikah
Only when you can
Bas etha/lamman tegdar *(etha is more common)*
They were without me yesterday
Hum kanu bdooni ams
Do I need to drive the car fast or slow?
Ahtaj Asoog al seyyara bsr'aa wala bel?
It is cold inside the library
Bard dakhel al-maktabah
Yes, I like to eat this hot for my lunch
Eih, ye'jebny akil haar bil-ghada
I can work today
Agdar asht'eghel alyom

*"Were" is *kanu*, but for "they were," "We were" is *kenna*.

*"I can" and "can I?" is *ana agdar*. "You can" or "can you?" is *ent tegdr?*

To answer – (M)Yejaweb (F) Tejaweb
To fly – Yeteer / Yesafer
Time / Times - Mrra / Mrrat
To travel – Yesafer
To learn - At'allam / (M) Yt'alam / (F) Tet'alam
How – Kif / Sh-loan
To swim - Asbah / (M) Yesbah / (F) Tesbah
To practice – Atmmarran
To play - Al'aab
To leave – Yemshi / Yetla'a / Ykhalli
Many /much /a lot – Ktheer / Wajed
I go to – Amshy / Arooh
First – Al-awl
Time / Times – Mrra/Mrrat

I want to answer many questions
Ana abe ajwaeb as'ila ktheera
I must fly to Dubai today
Ana lazim asafer Dubai alyom
I need to learn how to swim at the pool
Ana ahtaj at'allam kif asbah bil masbah
I want to learn to play better tennis
Abe at'allam al'aab tennis ahsan
I want to leave this here for you when I go to travel the world
Abe atrok hatha hena lk lamman arooh asafer al 'aalamm
Since the first time
Min awl mrra
The children are yours
Al-altfal haggonak

*In Saudi Gulf dialect, "to leave (something)" is (M)Yikhley /(F) Tkhaley/ Akhley. "To leave (a place)" is (M)Yet'la'/ (F) Tet'la'/ At'la'.

*In Gulf dialect, there are three definitions for time:
  - "time" / *mudda* refers to "era", "moment period," "duration of time."
  - "time(s)" / *marra(t)* /refers to "occasion" or "frequency."
  - "time" / *sa'a* references "hour," "what time is it?"
With the knowledge you've gained so far, now try to create your own sentences!

Nobody / anyone – Mahad / Ay ahad
Against - Dhed
Us – Ehna
To visit - Yzoor
Mom / Mother – Ommi / Yumma
To give – Ye'ty
Which – Ay / Ayt
To meet – Ytqabal / Ytlaga
Someone – Ahad
Just - Bass
To walk - Ytmasha
Around – Hawalin
Towards – Etejah
Than - Min
Nothing – Abad / Mafe shi / Wala shi

Something is better than nothing
Shai ahsan min wala shai
I am against him
Ana dheddah
Is there anyone here?
Fe ahad hena?
We go to visit my family each week
Nrooh nzoor al ahil kl asboo'
I need to give you something
Ahtaj a'atek shai
Do you want to go meet someone?
Taby tgabil ahad?
I was here on Wednesdays as well
Ana kent h ena al arba' ba'ad
Do you do every day
Ent tsawwy hatha kl youm?
You need to walk around, but not towards the house
Ent tehtaj tmshy, bass mub etjiah albait

*In Arabic, when using the pronoun "you" as a direct and indirect object pronoun (the person who is actually affected by the action that is being carried out) in relation to a verb, the pronoun "you" becomes a suffix to that verb. That suffix becomes *ak* (masc.) *ich* (fem.).

* "to give" / *a'te* "to give you" / *a'teek*
* "to tell" / *qool*: "to tell you" / qoolak (m.), Agool-lich (f.)
* "see you" / *ashoofak*: "to see you" (plural) / a*shoofkom* (m.), a*shoofkon* (f.)

For third person male, add *oh* and *hom* for plural, for female add h*a* and h*on* for plural.

* "tell him" / *gool-lah*
* "tell her" / *qool-lha*
* "see them" / *shoofhom* (m.), *shoofhon* (f.)
* "see us "/ *shoofna*

I have – 'Endy
Don't - La
Friend – Saheb / Sadeeg
To borrow – Yetsallaf
To look like / resemble – Yeshbah
Like (preposition) - Shbah
Grandfather – Jad
To want - Yaby
To stay – Yjles / Ybga / Yage'd
To continue – Ystamer
Way – T'areeg
I don't - Ana ma rah
To show - Yewarry
To prepare – Yessawy / yejjahiz
I am not going – Ana mub arooh

Do you want to look like Salim
Tbe tseer teshabah Salim
I want to borrow this book for my grandfather
Abe ate'eer hal ketab hag jaddy
I want to drive and to continue on this way to my house
Abe asooq w astamer 'ala hathak alt'areeg lain-baity
I have a friend there, that's why I want to stay in Riyadh
'andy saheb hnak, ashan ketha weddi agles bel-Riyadh
I am not going to see anyone here
Ana ma rah ashoof ahad hena
I need to show you how to prepare breakfast
Ahtaj awareek kif tessawy alfotoor
Why don't you have the book?
Laish ma e'ndak/ ma'ak al-ktab?
That is incorrect, I don't need the car today
Hatha ghalat, ana ma ahtaj alseyyara al-youm

*In Saudi Arabic the case of "you don't have" is *ma e'ndak* or *ma ma'ak* or *ma 'endy.*

To remember - 'Atthakkar
Your - (M) Tak / (F) tech
Number - Raqm
Hour - Sa'aa
Dark / darkness – Dhalam
About / on the - 'Ala
Grandmother - Jadda / my grandmother –Jaddateya
Five - Khams
Minute / minutes - Dqeeqa / Dqayq
More – Akthar
To think – Yfakker
To do – Yea'mel / Yessawy
To come – Yejy
To hear - Ysma'
Last – Akheer / Akher

You need to remember my number
Tehtaj tet'thakkar raqmy
This is the last hour of darkness
Hathy akher Sa'aa min al lail / aldhalam
**I want to come and to hear my grandmother speak Saudi
Arabic** Abe ajy w sma' jaddateya tetkalm 'araby Saudi
I need to think more about this, and what to do
Ahtaj afakker fe hatha akthar, w aiysh asawwy
From here to there, it's only five minutes
Min hena le hnak, bass khams dqayq
The school on the mountain
Almadrasa ala al jabal

To leave – Nkhroj / Netla'
Again – Ba'ad / Thanya
Arabic - Arabi
To take - Nakhth
To try – Ajreb / Ahawel
To rent – A'ajer
Without her - Bdonha
We are – Ehna
To turn off - Ytaffy
To ask – Ys'al
To stop - Ywqf
Permission - Ethn

He needs to leave and rent a house at the beach
Hw yhtaj ykhroj w y'ajer bait ala al shate'a
I want to take the test without her
Abe akth al emtehan bdonha
We are here a long time
Ehna hena min wagt toweel
I need to turn off the lights early tonight
Ahtaj at'afey alanwaar badry aleil
We want to stop here
Naby nwgaf hena
We are from Dammam
Ehna min al-dammam
The same building
Nafs alemara / almabna
I want to ask permission to leave
Ana abe ethn ashan atla'
I want to sleep
Ana abe anam

To open - Yeftah
A bit, a little, a little bit - Shway
To pay – Yedfa'
Once again – Mrra thanya
There isn't/ there aren't - Mafi
Sister - Ekht
To hope – Atmna
To live - Y'esh
Nice to meet you – Tsharafna
Name - Esm
Last name – Esm al 'ayla
To return – Yerja'
Door - Baab

I need to open the door for my sister
Ana ahtaj aftah elbaab l-okhty
I need to buy something
Ana ahtaj ashtrey shay
I want to meet your sisters
Ana abe ata'raf a'la okhtak.
Nice to meet you, what is your name and your last name
Tesharrafn, shenu esmak w esm 'eltak?
To hope for a little better
Tmna shwya ahsan
I want to return from the United States and to live in Qatar without problems
Abe arja' min America w a'eesh fe Qatar bdoon meshakel
Why are you sad right now?
'Lesh ent Hazeen / za'laan elhin?
There aren't any people here
Mafe nas hena
There isn't enough time to go to Qatif today
Mafe waqt kafy nmshy al Qatif al-youm

*In Saudi Arabic, regarding the verb "to meet" there are two separate cases to define this verb; *tqabil*. Depending of the context: to meet for business is *agabil* like in the sentence "do you want to go meet someone?" However, for meeting the sister, is getting acquainted with her, here it's tet'araf

*This *isn't* a phrase book! The purpose of this book is *solely* to provide you with the tools to create *your own* sentences!

To happen – Yeseer
To order – Yetlub
To drink -Yeshrab
Excuse me - (M) Law samaht / (F) Law smahati
Child - (M) T'efl (F) T'efla
Woman – Mra / Hurma
To begin / to start - Ybda
To finish - Yentahi
To help – Yesa'ed
To smoke - Yedakhen
To love - Yheb
To talk / to speak – Ytkallam
Gulf Cooperation Council – Majlis al-ta'aiwun al-khaliji

This must happen today
Hatha lazim yeseer l-yom
Excuse me, my child is here as well
Law samaht, ibny hena ba'ad
I love you
Ana ahebak (F) ahebich
I see you
Ana ashoofak (F) ashoofich
I need you at my side
Ahtajak janbi (F) Ahtajich
I need to begin soon to be able to finish at 3 o'clock in the afternoon
Ahtaj abda badri ashan agdar akhalles ala alsa'a 3 aldhuhr
I need help
Ahtaj mosa'ada
I don't want to smoke once again
Ana ma abe adakhen marra thanya
I want to learn how to speak Arabic
Abe at'allam kaif atkallam arabi

*"To be able to" is *agdar-word- ex. To be able to learn - agdar at'allam.*

To read - Yeqra
To write - Yektob
To teach – Y'allem
To close – Yegaffel
To choose - Yekhtar
To prefer - Yefaddill
To put - Yehott
Less - Agal
Sun - Shamss
Month - Shahr
I talk - Atkalm
Exact – Tamam / Bel-zhabt'

I need this book to learn how to read and write in Arabic because I want to teach in Egypt
Ahtaj hatha al-ktaab ashan at'allam kaif agra w aktob bel 'araby ashan abe addarres fe masser.
I want to close the door of the house
Abe assakker baab albeit
I prefer to put the gift here
afaddill ahott al hadeya hena
I want to pay less than you for the dinner
Abe adfaa' agal minnak lel-'asha
I speak with the boy and the girl in French
Ana atkalm ma' alwlad w albentt bill faransi
There is sun outside today
Fi shamss barra l-yom
Is it possible to know the exact date?
Momken te'aref alwaqt Bel-zhabt'?

*"For the" is *le al*

*"In" is *be al* / *fe al*

*With the knowledge you've gained so far, now try to create your own sentences!

To exchange (money**) –**Yehawwel
To call – Yenade
Brother – Akh
Dad – 'Ab
To sit – Yejles / Yag'ed
Together – Sawa / Ma' ba'adh
To change –Yeghayyer
Of course - Tab'an / Akeed
Welcome – Hala
During - Athna
Years - (**S**)'Aam / Sana / (**P**) 'A'waam / Sineen
Sky - Sama
Up – Foq
Down - Taht
Sorry - Aseff
To follow - Yelhag
To the – Le / Lain
Big – Kabeer
New – Jadeed
Never / ever - 'Omry ma / Abad / Ma gad

I don't want to exchange this money at the bank
Ana ma abe ahhawwel al flos fel-bank
I want to call my brother and my dad today
Ana abe 'akallim akhoy w aboy al-youm
Of course I can come to the theater, and I want to sit together with you and with your sister
Akeed agdar aje a'l massrah, w ana abe njles sawa ma'ak w ma' okhtak
I need to go down to see your new house
Abe arooh ashoof baytik al jdeed
I can see the sky from the window
Agdar ashof alsama min alnafetha/ aldreesha
I am sorry, but he wants to follow her to the store
Ana aseff, bas ho yabi yelhag'ha len almahal
I don't ever want to see you again
Ma abe ashofak Thanyea abad

*In Saudi Gulf dialect, brother is *akh,* and dad is *ab.* However, "my dad" is *abooy* and "my brother" is a*khoy.* "My sister" is e*khtey,* and "my mother" is *ommi*

*For the possessive pronouns, her (*ha*) and him (*ah*), both become suffixes to the verb or noun. Concerning nouns: her house / *baitha,* his house / *baitah* Concerning verbs please see page #19.

To allow - Yesmah
To believe – Yesaddeg
Morning – Sbaah
Except - Ma 'ada / Ella
To promise - Yw'ed
Good night – Tesbah ala khair
To recognize - Ye'araf
People - Naas
To move - Yharrek
Far - B'eed
Different – ghair
Man - rajjal
To enter - Yedkhal
To receive – Yestagbil / Yakhoth
Throughout – Min bain
Good evening – Masaa' alkheir
Left / right - Ysar / Ymeen

I need to allow him to go with us, he is a different man now
Ahtaj akhallih yeje m'aana, ho rajjal thany alhen
I believe everything except this
Ana asaddig kl shai ela hatha
I promise to say good night to my parents each night
Wa'ad eni agol tesbah ala khair le ahli kl laila
The people from Jordan are very pleasant
Alnas min alordon hlailen
I need to find another hotel very quickly
Ahtaj alga/ahhassel fondog thany bsr'aa
They need to receive a book for work
Hom yehtajoon yakhtho alkitab lel'amal
I see the sun in the morning
Ana ashoof alshams fil-sabah
The house is on the right side of the street
Albeit ala aljanb alyamen min alshare'

To wish - Atmanna
Bad – Saye'e
To get - Akhoth
To forget - Ansa
Everybody / Everyone - Kl shakhs
Although – Ma'a enna
To feel - Ahiss
Great – Zain
Next (as in close, near) - Janb
Next (as in next year) - Jai
To like – A'ajab
In front – Qeddam
Person - Shakhs
Behind – Khalf / Wara
Well – Zain / Kuwaies
Restaurant – Mata'am
Bathroom – Hammam
Goodbye – Ma' alsalama

I don't want to wish you anything bad
Ana ma atmana lak ay shay mo zaina
I must forget everybody from my past to feel well
Ana bansa kl shaks min al madhy a'shan ahess ahsan
I am next to the person behind you
Ana janb al shakhs ally warak
There is a great person in front of me
Fi shakhs a'dheem gedammy
I say goodbye to my friends
Ana aqoul ma' alsalama l asdega'e
Where is the bathroom in the restaurant?
Wain alhammam bill mata'am?
She has to get a car before the next year
He lazim tjeb seyyara qabl alsana al jaia
I like the house, but it is very small
Ajbni albeit, bass marra sagher

*janb literally means "side." In Arabic, it refers to "next." janb is "besides me" and janbak is "besides you."

To remove / to take out - Yeshel
Please - Takfa
Beautiful - (**M**)Mzyon, (**F**)Jameela
To lift – Yerfa'
Include / Including - Yeshmal
Belong – Yantami le
To hold - Yemsak
To check – Yeraje' / Yeta'akad
Small – Sagheer
Real - Haqeeqy
Week – Esboo'
Size – Hajm / Magas
Even though – Hatta law
Doesn't – Ma
So (as in "then") **–** Ya'ny / W baa'den
So (as in "so big") – Marra / Heel
Price – Thaman / Se'er

She wants to remove this door please
He taby tsheel ha-albab law samaht
This doesn't belong here, I need to check again
Hatha mkanh mu hna, ahtaj at'akad mrra thanya
This week the weather was very beautiful
Hatha alesboo' aljaw heel helo
I need to know which is the real diamond
Ahtaj a'aref ay almasa el-hqeeqya
We need to check the size of the house
Nehtaj neshoof hajm albait
I want to lift this, so you need to hold it high
Abe ashel hatha, ya'ny lazim temsakah fog
I can pay this even though that the price is expensive
Agdar adfa' hatha hatta law alse'er ghali
Including everything is this price correct?
Shamel kl shi hatha alse'er sah?

Countries of the Middle East
Duoal al-sharq al- awsatt

Lebanon - Lobnan
Syria - Suriyya
Jordan - L-ordon
Saudi Arabia - al-so'odya
Israel /Palestine /West Bank -
Isra'eel / Falasteen / al-daffa
algharbiyya
Bahrain - l-Bahrein
Yemen - l-Yaman
Oman - 'Oman
United Arab Emirates - l-Emarat
al'arabya el-motaheda
Kuwait - l-Kwait
Iraq - l-Iraq
Qatar - Qatar
Morocco - al-maghreb
Algeria - l-Jazayer
Libya - Leebya
Egypt - Masser
Tunisia – Tunes

Months
January - ynayr
February - febrayr
March – mares
April - ebreel
May - may
June – Yuniu
July – Yuliu
August - aughustus
September – September
October - oktobar
November - november
December - december

Colors
Black - aswad
White - abyadh
Gray - Rmaddi
Red - ahamr
Blue - azraq
Yellow - asfar
Green - akhdhar
Orange – brtgali
Purple - banfsaji
Brown –bonni

Numbers
One - Wahed
Two - thnen
Three – Thlath
Four - arb'aa
Five – Khams
Six - Sitt
Seven - Sab'a
Eight - Thman
Nine – Tis'a
Ten - 'Ashr
Twenty - 'Eshreen
Thirty - Thlathen
Thirty - Talateen
Forty - Arb'in
Fifty - Khamseen
Sixty - Sitteen
Seventy - Sab'een
Eighty - Tamaneen
Ninety - Tis'een
Hundred - Miyya
Thousand – Alf
Million - Million

Days of the Week
Sunday - al- ahad
Monday - al-athnen
Tuesday - al-tholatha'
Wednesday - al-arbe'aa'
Thursday - al-khamees
Friday - jom'aa
Saturday – Sabt

Seasons
Spring – Rabee'
Summer - Seif
Autumn - Khareef
Winter - Shetta

Cardinal Directions
North - Shamaal
South - Janoob
East – Sharq
West - Gharb

Conclusion

Congratulations! You have completed all the tools needed to master the Najdi, Hijazi, and the Saudi Gulf dialects and I hope that this has been a valuable learning experience. Now you have sufficient communication skills to be confident enough to embark on a visit to the Kingdom of Saudi Arabian, impress your friends, and boost your resume so *good luck.*

This program is available in other languages as well, and it is my fervent hope that my language learning programs will be used for good, enabling people from all corners of the globe and from all cultures and religions to be able to communicate harmoniously. After memorizing the required three hundred and fifty words, please perform a daily five-minute exercise by creating sentences in your head using these words. This simple exercise will help you grasp conversational communications even more effectively. Also, once you memorize the vocabulary on each page, follow it by using a notecard to cover the words you have just memorized and test yourself and follow *that* by going back and using this same notecard technique on the pages you studied during the previous days. This repetition technique will assist you in mastering these words in order to provide you with the tools to create your own sentences.

Every day, use this notecard technique on the words that you have just studied.

Everything in life has a catch. The catch here is just consistency. If you just open the book, and after the first few pages of studying the program, you put it down, then you will not gain anything. However, if you consistently dedicate a half hour daily to studying, as well as reviewing what you have learned from previous days, then you will quickly realize why this method is the most effective technique ever created to become conversational in a foreign language. My technique works! For anyone who doubts this technique, all I can say is that it has worked for me and hundreds of others.

NOTE FROM THE AUTHOR

Thank you for your interest in my work. I encourage you to share your overall experience of this book by posting a review. Your review can make a difference! Please feel free to describe how you benefited from my method or provide creative feedback on how I can improve this program. I am constantly seeking ways to enhance the quality of this product, based on personal testimonials and suggestions from individuals like you. In order to post a review, please check with the retailer of this book.

Thanks and best of luck,

Yatir Nitzany